The Cocker Spaniel

Dennis McCarthy

Illustrations by Sheila Smith

John Bartholomew & Son Limited
Edinburgh

First published in Great Britain 1980 by
JOHN BARTHOLOMEW & SON LIMITED,
12 Duncan Street, Edinburgh, EH9 1TA.

ISBN 0 7028 8370 0

McCarthy, Dennis
The Cocker Spaniel, (Bartholomew Pet Series)
1. Cocker Spaniels
I. Title
636.7'52   SF429.C55

Printed in Great Britain by
John Bartholomew & Son Limited, Edinburgh.

Contents

Golden Cocker Spaniel

The History of the Breed

One of the problems about sorting out the Cocker Spaniel's history is that up to about 1800 many breeds of Field dogs came under one heading — Spaniels. The 'Cocking Spaniel' was named as early as the beginning of the 19th century, but the Cocker Spaniel as such was not registered at the English Kennel Club until 1893. We have probable mention of the dog we know as the Cocker today as early as the 14th century, but the difficulty of pinpointing the early history of the breed lies in the fact that a Spaniel of under 25lb (11.3kg) was often called a 'Cocker'. The limit of this weight was abolished in 1901 — a good thing too — because in the same litter you could find a Cocker Spaniel — if it was under 25lb (11.3kg) — and a Springer Spaniel if it was over 25lb (11.3kg).

Chaucer was kind enough to write about a Spaniel closely resembling the Cocker in the 14th century, and other writers mentioned a Field dog used for falconry in the 15th and 16th centuries. Almost certainly this was a Cocker — or at least 'Cocker type' — a phrase that present-day breeders would detest.

By legend a Cocker Spaniel was aboard the *Mayflower* when the Pilgrim Fathers sailed to America from Southampton in 1620. No amount of research will find that Cocker in the cargo list of the *Mayflower* but why doubt the legend? The Cocker would have been a fine companion and a useful dog for the first British settlers in the New World.

It is accepted that the Cocker Spaniel got its name because of its close association with the Woodcock, and an early name for the breed was 'Wood-Cocker'. It is also accepted that the Cocker is a dog of Spaniel mixture up to the beginning of this century. Whether today's breeders like it or not, the present Cocker owes its size, habits, colouring and shape to other breeds of Field Spaniels being mixed together about one hundred years ago. The crossing of Cockers and Sussex Spaniels was openly done a hundred years ago, but it would be unthinkable today to mix what we regard as 'pure' blood with any other.

As an example of the variance in the Cocker Spaniel type, at one time in England a large number of so-called Cocker Spaniels were quite probably other breeds. It is known that small Field Spaniels found their way into shows under the classification of Cockers. There were also Devonshire Cockers and Welsh Cockers and there is evidence that other parts of England had developed their own type of Cockers. The founding of the Cocker Spaniel Club in 1902 went a long way to encouraging the develop- ment of the type of Cocker we know today, though early photo- graphs sometimes show a dog with a markedly longer back than is now accepted. When Cockers were officially recognized they were not as smartly turned out as we see today, but the Cocker seems always to have been a neat dog — unlike many coated breeds that were often shown in a matted condition and some- times sparsely coated at the early part of this century.

The Spaniel Club was formed in 1885, but seventeen years later when the Cocker Spaniel Club was founded the breed became popular at dog shows, though at this time many Cocker breeders used their dogs only in the field and the thought of showing off their beauty points was not foremost in their minds.

The Cocker has become an important show dog and pet. When registrations at the English Kennel Club became a requirement for the Cocker to be recognized properly as a true specimen of the breed there were just a handful of dogs listed. In 1914, 400 registrations were made. In the 1920s and 1930s the registrations went up by leaps and bounds and the Cockers always lead the Spaniel registration table. In 1929, 685 Cockers exhibited at Cruft's Dog Show — fifty years later, in 1979, only 129 Cockers were present but by then there were restrictions on entry.

In 1939, 5,372 Cockers were registered and after the Second World War, in 1947, 27,000 were recorded. Today's breeders would throw up their hands in horror at that figure — it smacks of indiscriminate breeding and of breeding purely for profit, ignoring breed characteristics and the importance of pedigrees. A great deal of harm was done to the breed in those early post-war years and temperament particularly suffered. Many top winning dogs at the time had such mixed up pedigrees that they were impossible to follow. It was some years before the Cocker Spaniel got itself in order again.

The Cocker was not alone in this post-war boom and resultant bad breeding. Other popular breeds of the day suffered and it took many years and several generations of better breeding to get back to normal again. In 1950 the Cocker registration figure in Britain was 16,226 but within two years it was down to a more sensible four figures (9,854) and it settled into a norm of five to six thousand a year until 1976 when a new type of registration came into effect. In 1976 3,336 Cockers were registered because it became more expensive to register puppies at The Kennel Club with dogs being recorded in the Annual Register for 'Competition, Breeding and Export Purposes' — and none of these categories account for the pet Cocker. So up to 1976 the registration figures gave a good indication of the number of Cockers being bred in Britain — after this time the figures are no longer reliable.

According to keen breed researchers we owe today's Cocker Spaniel to a dog named Bob, born of a black and tan named Frank and a black and white mother named Venus around 1855.

The most famous Cocker of all time is reckoned to be a dog named Obo — his sire was a Sussex Spaniel and his dam a Field Spaniel. His son, Obo II, was a famous dog in Canada and eventually he went to America. He was a smallish dog but he is behind nearly all the American Cockers.

Like so many breeds of dogs the Cocker Spaniel's history is shrouded in mystery. He was, undoubtedly, man-made but he is not to earn less respect for this. Most breeds are similarly man-made, and there are very few dogs that claim to be 'pure' and natural.

Breed enthusiasts are often anxious to try to prove their dogs have ancient ancestry. Writers throughout the ages have mentioned dogs used with hawking and hunting. Whether these were always Spaniels, as we know the group-meaning today, or Cockers, to be specific, is open to speculation. I read a very good and interesting Cocker book recently where the author had obviously done a great deal of research into ancient writings, picking up little gems from over a thousand years ago. Whether it is always safe to assume that it is the Cocker being written about I would not like to say, but early pictures and engravings do add evidence to a strong Cocker-type dog being used in the field.

I have been fortunate enough to travel to many countries judging dogs and I always think of the Cocker as being as British as the Bulldog. Certainly British breeders developed the Cocker to a high degree of efficiency both in the field and in the show ring.

It has never been properly sorted out about that word 'Spaniel'. In a sporting book written in the 15th century the author proclaimed that Spaniels came from Spain. It is all very puzzling to the present-day student to sort out fanciful fiction from fact. Perhaps it is enough to say that the Cocker Spaniel has been with us in some shape, size or form for many centuries!

In the early years of this century American imports are remembered by old and wise breeders, so something must have been stirring in the Cocker world in the U.S.A. in the 19th century. Breeders at the turn of the century were generally known to be stricter than some today in their breeding selection, and the American imports into Britain must have had a little more than average to recommend them.

The Cocker over the years has had noble patronage. In the 19th century when there was hunting, fishing and shooting on a large scale on the huge estates of the Dukes and Lords of the Kingdom, it would be unthinkable to go out into the field without a Cocker. Their ownership was usually distinguishable by colour. The Duke of Such and Such would have blue roans; Lord Whatsit would have black and tans, and so on. Reading of the old days it seems one needed a Peerage to own a Cocker!

Since the Spaniel Club was formed, specialist clubs for Cocker Spaniel devotees have sprung up all over the world. There are thirty in Britain now, many more in America, and others in nearly every country. In addition there are Spaniel clubs that incorporate an interest in the Cocker, and there are Gundog clubs that similarly include Cockers on their roll. The Cocker owner has a great choice of clubs to join and gain further information about the breed. Many Cocker clubs specialize in certain colours, going back to the days when there really was colour prejudice and some colours were hardly ever placed at a dog show.

Since personnel of the breed clubs tend to change, if you want information about a Cocker club near to you, write to The Kennel Club.

From the beginning of Cocker registrations up to the First World War parti-colour Cockers were popular, and obviously breeders were more concerned about type and breed characteristics than colour. Black, black and tan, black and white and blue roan were very popular colour combinations. Then in the 1920s the reds and goldens achieved some popularity with the formation of their own specialist club.

During the years of the Second World War the breeding of dogs was almost at a standstill due to the problems of transport and obtaining regular food supplies, but after the war breeding started up again in a very big way, and the popularity of the Cocker as a very loving companion of a useful size with a good degree of obedience brought that huge increase in registrations.

I mentioned that the 1920s saw the formation of a club for red and golden Cockers, but the red traces its history back to the 1890s when a red Cocker was imported into England from America. At that time several black dogs had red in their breeding and they produced reds. Twenty-four breeders formed the Red and Golden Cocker Spaniel Club and it is said that at that time there was open prejudice against the colours in the breed. It would be a pretence to say there is no colour prejudice today. People do have colour preference. There is no law against this, but it is unfortunate when a judge goes into a show ring prejudiced against certain colours. It happens at shows of all sizes but it is obviously wrong for a Cocker to be marked down on colour alone.

In the early days of the Cocker, blacks were evidently fairly rare, and the original colour was either liver and tan or black and tan. These colours are still with us today, of course.

It is strange that at one time certain faults were associated with colour. Some early reds and goldens were described at the time as having frowns, curly coats and too much throat, and some were said to have temperament problems. It would be unfair to penalize coloured Cockers these days with specific faults that obviously were there in the years between the two World Wars.

The history of showing dogs goes back to June 1859 at Newcastle-upon-Tyne with a show organized for just Pointers and Setters. Within a few years other breeds joined that privileged twosome and dog shows sprang up everywhere. There was a dog show held before that date that recently came to light. To be more precise it was a dog and cat show! 'The Prize Dog and Cat Show' was held in the drawing room in a house in London's Mayfair district in February 1846 and the 6th prize went to Flora — 'a beautiful little Spaniel who was warranted to stand at a carriage window two hours at one sitting. It had walked all the way upstairs. Fed by Miss Pamby's page off broken victuals and maids of honour'. Before you get over-excited about that Spaniel winning a prize at what must have been the very first show in the world, I must tell you that it is believed to have been beaten into 6th place by two cats!

Over the years Cockers have made news. In 1958 Tom Shrewbridge, a rancher, left an estate in California and shares in the San José Water Works to his Cocker, George. I have no idea how George managed his legacy, but it was worth a cool 100,000 dollars.

This book is essentially about the English Cocker Spaniel, but I must make mention of the American Cocker Spaniel. In 1970 the English Kennel Club recognized the American Cocker Spaniel. They could hardly have done otherwise. In the 1960s the American Cocker invaded Britain in some numbers, by way of Holland. I well remember a very famous English Cocker Spaniel breeder saying he wouldn't have this dreadful dog in his kennel! Within five years he had American Cockers and was showing and breeding them extensively.

What a charmer! There really must be something very special about the American Cocker. At one time no one in Britain would have dared to have taken this glamorous dog in the field but the first two full Champions have now been made up. Owned by Mr. Wylde and working with great enthusiasm at a Field Trial in plastic coats they won their Field Trial Champion title to add to their Show Champion title.

There is interest in obedience tests with American Cockers in England, and in the U.S.A. the American Cocker Obedience Champions have already hit the headlines. Trust the American breeders to create a dog that is essentially a showman from unlikely stock. While the Cocker has much charm, it is mainly a working dog and while you might say a Cocker is a handsome dog, the word 'glamorous' is really too effeminate for such a dog, but the American breeders created this glamorous dog and it is certainly not effeminate.

The Americans changed the shape of the head, shortened the back, increased the length of the neck and encouraged the growth of coat — a lot of coat. In other words, everything about the English Cocker was exaggerated to create the American Cocker Spaniel.

We think today of the American as having a good temperament and yet that great American judge, Mrs. C. Bede Maxwell, writing in her book *The Truth About Sporting Dogs,* said she was always warned that the first dog to bite her in the show ring would be an American Cocker Spaniel, and sure enough an eight month old one obliged!

Mrs. Maxwell was the first to judge American Cocker Spaniel classes at a British show and in no time at all the American was winning top awards at shows all over Britain. It is now accepted as a distinct breed by everyone. After the European mainland was conquered by the Americans — and then Britain — it was not long before the American Cocker captured the hearts of Australian and New Zealand breeders.

I remember seeing a good number of American Cockers at a show in Amsterdam in the 1960s — unlike other 'glamorous' breeds that the continentals seemed to have some difficulty in grooming to British standards, the American was groomed and put down in the ring beautifully. I thought then it would not be long before he became popular in Britain. I was not far wrong.

Just as the English Cocker owes his development to a mixture of breeds — and the honest Cocker enthusiast will admit that the mixture of breeds was sometimes deliberate and probably happened occasionally by accident — the American Cocker was similarly created. The development of the American Cocker we

13

know today started in the 1920s and forged ahead prominently in the 1930s. You would have difficulty in finding a mention in dog books written by British scribes at the time, but in America the 'Yankee' as he was affectionately called was creating an impression in the show ring. We may never know his true make-up of ancestry. In an effort to get colour and coat — a lot of coat — the breeders obviously put quite a mixture of breeds together and did not always advertise the fact. Some Toy Spaniel certainly was used and helped to develop the typical Yankee head and eye, and small-sized Cockers are in there somewhere together with the Field Spaniel. Oh! it is a right mixture, but the end product is a dog with much character and warmth.

When early exports were made from America really good stock was sent abroad and arrived in the host country in good condition and well representing top American breeding. In so many other breeds poor specimens were exported to other countries. I can remember when I first bred a litter and received enquiries from abroad, I was told by a very famous breeder of the day never, but never, to consider sending the best out of the country. Second-rate stock is good enough for export.

Superb American Cockers landed in England from America and the Continent and justifiably the American Cocker gained an immediate place in the affection and support of top breeders and exhibitors.

The Breed Standard

Each breed of dog has a Breed Standard, which is really the blue-print of the perfect dog. Old and wise breeders will tell you that the perfect dog has yet to be born, so a Breed Standard has to be looked at as an indicator of desired breed points. If your dog fails miserably according to the Standard you might be surprised how well he might do in the show ring, and yet the Breed Standard is really for show ring purposes! In the field the Breed Standard is of little use, and I might say here that often the Breed Standard is of little use in the home, since temperament is the all important point if you have to live with your dog.

I think it is of interest that soon after the foundation of the Cocker Spaniel Club in 1902 a scale of points as well as a 'standard' of points was laid down for the Cocker. It was obviously to assist judges and in the late 1930s this scale of points was still mentioned in various dog books. Probably because judges — particularly breeder/judges — felt that this scale of points was restricting the development of desirable breed points, they faded away soon after the Second World War and any judge using a scale of points today would be looked at very strangely. However, these scales of points are of interest because they show what breeders were aiming for in the early part of this century. In truth, if we have departed from these early Cockers, have we not departed from the true dog?

The scale of points for the Cocker Spaniel at the turn of the century was as follows:

Positive points:

Head and jaws	10
Eyes	5
Ears	5
Neck	10
Body	20
Forelegs	10
Hind legs	10
Feet	10
Stern	10
Coat and feather	10
Total: *Positive points*	**100**

Negative points:

Light eyes	10
Light nose	15
Hair curled on ears (very undesirable)	15
Coat (curly, woolly or wiry)	20
Carriage of stern	20
Topknot	20
Total: *Negative points*	**100**

Strange that the 'very undesirable' curly hair on the ears listed only 15 points against the 20 points of the stern carriage, and topknot but, of course, a curly coat on the ears and on the legs and body gave 35 negative points, and I should think that was the end of the dog in the show ring! But I wonder whether judging to a strict scale of points like this might produce more consistent results and — dare I say it — fairer judging? In my view the show ring is no place for the judge who awards prizes on fads and fancies. There is a Breed Standard which has to be accepted — why not the back-up of a scale of points approved by the breed clubs and The Kennel Club? It would stop the bias against colour which still finds its way into a judge's awards. It might also be of assistance to novice judges with limited experience of the finer points of Cockers. The scale of points might assist judges in finding 'good, honest dogs' rather than wins given to dogs who are popular winners of the day.

The Breed Standards were begun a long time ago — at the beginning of organized dog shows around 1865 a standard of points was in existence for the fashionable dogs of the day. As breed clubs came into existence, The Kennel Club liased with their leading members to form official Breed Standards, though the first mention of a Breed Standard for the Cocker was listed as: 'Standard of Points for the Black Cocker Spaniel' and there was another list 'Standard of Points for Any Other Variety Cocker Spaniel' which allowed for other colours!

The Cocker Spaniel Standard in use today was last amended in 1969, when selected breeders got together to propose recommendations to The Kennel Club.

The Cocker Spaniel: The British Standard — Reproduced by permission of The Kennel Club

General appearance: That of a merry sturdy sporting dog. The Cocker Spaniel should be well-balanced and compact and should measure about the same from the withers to the ground as from the withers to the root of the tail.

Head and skull: There should be a good square muzzle with a distinct stop which should be midway between the tip of the nose and the occiput. The skull should be well-developed, cleanly chiselled, neither too fine nor too coarse. The cheek-bones should not be prominent. The nose should be sufficiently wide to allow for the acute scenting power of this breed.

Eyes: The eyes should be full but not prominent, brown or dark brown in colour, but never light, with a general expression of intelligence and gentleness though decidedly wide awake, bright and merry. The rims should be tight.

Ears: Lobular, set on low, on a level with the eyes, with fine leathers which extend to but not beyond the tip of the nose; well-clothed with long silky hair which should be straight.

Mouth: Jaws should be strong and teeth should have a scissor bite.

Neck: Neck should be moderate in length, clean in throat, muscular and neatly set into fine sloping shoulders.

Forequarters: The shoulders should be sloping and fine, the chest well-developed and the brisket deep, neither too wide nor too narrow in front. The legs must be well-boned, feathered and straight, and should be sufficiently short for concentrated power but not too short to interfere with the tremendous exertions expected from this grand little sporting dog.

Body: Body should be immensely strong and compact for the size and weight of the dog. The ribs should be well-sprung behind the shoulder-blades, the loin short, wide and strong, with a firm topline gently sloping downwards to the tail.

Hindquarters: Hindquarters should be wide, well-rounded and very muscular. The legs must be well-boned, feathered to the hock, with a good bend of stifle and short below the hock allowing for plenty of drive.

Feet: Feet should be firm, thickly padded and cat-like.

Tail: Tail should be set on slightly lower than the line of the back; it must be merry, and never cocked up. The tail should not be docked too long nor too short to interfere with its merry action.

Coat: Flat and silky in texture, never wiry or wavy, with sufficient feather; not too profuse and never curly.

Colour: Various. In self-colours no white is allowed except on the chest.

Gait: There should be true through-action both fore and aft with great drive covering the ground well.

Weight and size: The weight should be about 28lb (12.7kg) to 32lb (14.5kg). The height at the withers should be approximately 15in (381mm) to 15½in (394mm) for bitches and approximately 15½in (394mm) to 16in (406mm) for dogs.

Faults: Light bone; straight shoulder; flat ribs; unsound movement; weak hocks; weak pasterns; open or large feet; frown; small beady eyes; undershot or overshot mouth; uncertain or aggressive temperament.

An ideal British Cocker Spaniel

Breed Standards *are* important — make no mistake about that. They come about after much soul-searching and painstaking argument and, sometimes, compromise. They should be read by every judge before he enters the ring to award prizes. But, in truth, when you see some show results you really wonder whether two judges are adhering to the same Breed Standard and you cannot be blamed for asking if one winning dog at one show is correct, then another winning dog at another show cannot be right. It is, of course, all a matter of interpretation. That is probably why compilers of the Breed Standards avoid being too specific and detailed about weight and size and precise measurement of the head, etc.

I think the Cocker Spaniel Breed Standard is a good one, and much better than the ones for some breeds.

I would like a dull coat to be listed as a fault. You might think good condition should be taken for granted but I remember a novice judge putting up a Cocker with a very dull coat and to my eye it was obviously not in good condition. When he asked me what I thought of his judging I told him so. He argued — there is no mention in the Standard of a dull coat being penalized! Well, I ask you! The compilers of the Standard would squirm if they knew their omission would bring forward that sort of comment from a judge claiming to have their Breed Standard in mind when he entered the show ring.

The word 'merry' is the one word which to my mind describes the dog perfectly and is more helpful than some other Breed Standards which do not even mention temperament.

The whole thing about the Cocker is balance. If you look at a dog and it does not seem to balance, you have seen the fault, whatever it is. The head is the first point to be looked at and while the Standard description is a good one I do feel that the head must be taken in balance with the rest of the dog. One always wants to avoid coarseness in a dog, but some dogs are of a heavier build than others, and this is acceptable. After all, the Cocker is a working dog and over-refinement, which some might regard as elegance, is wrong to my thinking.

The Cocker should be judged as a whole, and not in pieces or sections just because the Breed Standard is written that way. I plead for judges to go for a balanced dog — an honest all-round dog rather than a dog with a superb head and little else to recommend it. I am interested that the Standard says the teeth should have a scissor bite. Many other Breed Standards call for 'a level bite' and yet if you take that literally it surely means that the upper front jaw is exactly level with the lower front jaw. The only breed I have ever seen in some quantity with a true 'level' bite is the cocker! Most other breeds have a 'scissor' bite with the upper front teeth resting slightly over the lower front teeth, and yet their Standards call for a level bite and the Cocker Standard calls for a scissor bite.

The tail of the Cocker is a problem to sort out for the judge who has not had a great deal of experience of the breed. How much should a tail that is not carried 'merrily' be penalized? I remember judging a young Cocker once in a mixed breed class at a small show and I marked it down because its tail was clamped down. The breeder had a good go at me afterwards, saying I was wrong to fault it so strictly. I stuck to my guns and pointed out the 'merry action' of the Cocker listed in the Breed Standard. I was told not to take this too literally. I think I might have waivered a little with my assertion but I knew I was right with this particular dog because its rear movement was being badly affected by its clamped tail. Generally speaking the tail is a good indication of temperament. A clamped tail usually indicates a nervous dog and I think this should be penalized. The Cocker was created as a separate and distinct breed to work with the gun. How can you have a nervous dog in that environment?

The weight of the Cocker Spaniel has been fairly important in its development. After all, the weight at one time determined whether it be called a Cocker or Springer Spaniel. Up to 1950 the weight in the Standard was given as 25lb (11.3kg) to 28lb (12.7kg). In the amended 1969 Standard the weight went up to 28lb (12.7kg) to 32lb (14.5kg). The problem is you can only estimate the weight. The first judge to call for weighing scales to weigh a dog he thought did not fit into the weight requirements would be thought very odd.

The height allowance of a variation of ½in (12.7mm) must surely not be taken too seriously. I have seen taller and shorter

Cockers win top awards under specialist breed judges. All this is very puzzling to the novice judge at the ringside with the Breed Standard in his hands.

I must not be too critical of the Cocker Breed Standard, for as I have said it must be a matter of compromise on some points. Just as the perfect dog has yet to be born, I might say the perfect Breed Standard has yet to be devised.

Do not shoot your Cocker if it does not appear to be as perfect as the Breed Standard demands. If that tail wags when you come home after a hard day's work you may have a much better companion than the owner whose dog wins the major award at the top Championship show. The value of a dog has nothing to do with the Breed Standard really. The true value is what that dog means to you.

There is nothing in the Breed Standard about colour preference, and I do wish all judges would make a mental note of that when entering the show ring and judging Cockers. Having said that, it is sometimes a problem when a dog has marking on the head that particularly detracts from the expression or appears to change the shape of the head or muzzle. You might think that a strange thing to say, but I have seen patches of colour that certainly spoiled the appearance of the dog and I have never known whether to penalize a dog for this in the show ring. The ringsiders may be quite vocal in discussion about 'unfortunate' marking, but there is nothing in the Standard penalizing colour markings apart from allowing white only on the chest in self-colours.

I think it would be most helpful to newcomers to a breed if more clubs had discussions on interpretation of the Breed Standard.

The Breed Standard of the American Cocker is much fuller than that of his English cousin.

The American Cocker Spaniel: The Standard — Reproduced by permission of The Kennel Club

General appearance: A serviceable-looking dog with a refined chiselled head; standing on straight legs and well up at the shoulders; of compact body and wide, muscular quarters. The American Cocker Spaniel's sturdy body, powerful quarters and strong, well-boned legs show him to be a dog capable of considerable speed combined with great endurance. Above all he must be free and merry, sound, well-balanced throughout, and in action show a keen inclination to work, equable in temperament with no suggestion of timidity.

Head and skull: Well-developed and rounded with no tendency towards flatness, or pronounced roundness, of the crown (dome). The forehead smooth, that is, free from wrinkles, the eyebrows and stop clearly defined, the median line distinctly marked and gradually disappearing until lost rather more than half way up to the crown. The bony structure surrounding the socket of the eye should be well-chiselled; there should be no suggestion of fullness under the eyes nor prominence in the cheeks which, like the sides of the muzzle, should present a smooth, clean-cut appearance. To attain a well-proportioned head, which above all should be in balance with the rest of the dog, the distance from the tip of the nose to the stop at a line drawn across the top of the muzzle between the front corners of the eyes, should approximate one-half the distance from the stop at this point up over the crown to the base of the skull. The muzzle should be broad and deep, with square even jaws. The upper lip should be of sufficient depth to cover the lower jaw, presenting a square appearance. The nose of sufficient size to balance the muzzle and foreface, with well-developed nostrils and black in colour in the blacks and black and tans; in the reds, buffs, livers and parti-colours and in the roans it may be black or brown, the darker colouring being preferable.

Mouth: The teeth should be sound and regular and set at right angles to their respective jaws. The relation of the upper teeth to the lower teeth should be that of scissors, with the inner surface of the upper in contact with the outer surface of the lower when the jaws are closed.

Eyes: The eyeballs should be round and full and set in the surrounding tissue to look directly forward and give the eye a slightly almond-shape appearance. The eye should be neither weak nor goggled. The expression should be intelligent, alert, soft and appealing. The colour of the iris should be dark brown to black in the blacks, black and tans, buffs and creams, and in the darker shades of the parti-colours and roans. In the reds, dark hazel; in the livers, parti-colours, and roans of the lighter shades, not lighter than hazel, the darker the better.

Ears: Lobular, set on a line no higher than the lower part of the eye, the feathers fine and extending to the nostrils; well-clothed with long, silky, straight or wavy hair.

Neck: The neck should be sufficiently long to allow the nose to reach the ground easily, muscular and free from pendulous 'throatiness'. It should rise strongly from the shoulders and arch slightly as it tapers to join the head.

Forequarters: The shoulders deep, clean-cut and sloping without protrusion and so set that the upper point of the withers are at an angle which commits a wide spring of rib. Forelegs straight, strongly boned and muscular, and set close to the body well under the scapulae. The elbows well let down and turning neither in nor out. The pasterns short and strong.

Body: Its height at the withers should approximate the length from the withers to the set-on of tail. The chest deep, its lowest point no higher than the elbows, its front sufficiently wide for adequate heart and lung space, yet not so wide as to interfere with straightforward movement of the forelegs. Ribs deep and well-sprung throughout. Body short in the couplings and flank, with its depth at the flank somewhat less than at the last rib. Back strong and sloping evenly and slightly downward from the withers to the set-on of tail. Hips wide with quarters well-rounded and muscular. The body should appear short, compact and firmly knit together, giving the impression of strength.

Hindquarters: The hind legs should be strongly boned and muscled with good angulation at the stifle and powerful, clearly defined thighs. The stifle joint should be strong and there should be no slippage in motion or when standing. The hocks should be strong, well let down and when viewed from behind, the hind legs should be parallel when in motion and at rest.

Feet: Feet compact, not spreading, round and firm, with deep, strong, tough pads and hair between the toes; they should turn neither in nor out.

Gait: The American Cocker Spaniel possesses a typical sporting dog gait. Prerequisite to good movement is balance between the fore and hindquarters. He drives with his strong powerful rear quarters and is properly constructed to the shoulder and forelegs so that he can reach forward without constriction in a full stride to counter-balance the driving force of the rear. Above all, his gait is co-ordinated, smooth and effortless. The dog must cover ground with his action and excessive animation should never be mistaken for proper gait.

Tail: The docked tail should be set on and carried on a line with the topline of the back, or slightly higher; never straight up like a terrier and never so low as to indicate timidity. When the dog is in motion the action should be merry.

Coat: On the head, short and fine; on the body, medium length, with enough undercoating to give protection. The ears, chest, abdomen and legs should be well-feathered but not so excessively as to hide the American Cocker Spaniel's true lines and movement or affect his appearance and function as a sporting dog. The texture is most important. The coat should be silky, flat or slightly wavy, and of a texture which permits easy care. Excessive, curly or cottony texture coat should be penalized.

Colour: Blacks should be jet black; shadings of brown or liver in the sheen of the coat is not desirable. Black and tan (classified under solid colours) should have definite tan markings on a jet black body. The tan markings should be distinct and plainly visible and the colour of the tan may be from the lightest cream to the darkest red colour. The amount of tan markings should be restricted to ten per cent or less of the colour of the specimen; tan markings in excess of ten per cent should be penalized. Tan markings which are not readily visible in the ring or the absence of tan markings in any of the specified locations should be penalized. The tan markings should be located as follows:

1 A clear spot over each eye.
2 On the sides of the muzzle and on the cheeks.
3 On the undersides of the ears.
4 On all feet and legs.
5 Under the tail.
6 On the chest, optional: presence or absence should not be penalized.

Tan on the muzzle which extends upwards over and joins should be penalized.
Any solid colour other than black should be of uniform shade. Lighter colouring of the feathering is permissable.
In all the above solid colours a small amount of white on chest and throat (while not desirable) is allowed, but white in any other location should be penalized.

Parti-colours — two or more definite colours appearing in clearly defined markings are essential. Primary colour which is ninety per cent or more should be penalized: secondary colour or colours which are limited solely to one location should also be penalized. Roans are classified as parti-colours and may be of any of the usual roaning patterns.

Tri-colours — any of the above colours combined with tan markings. It is preferable that the tan markings be located in the same pattern as for black and tans.

Size: The ideal height at the withers for an adult dog is 15in (381mm), and for an adult bitch 14in (356mm). Height may vary a half inch above or below this ideal. A dog whose height exceeds 15½in (394mm), or a bitch whose height exceeds 14½in (369mm), should be penalized. An adult dog whose height is less than 14½in (369mm), or an adult bitch whose height is less than 13½in (343mm), should be penalized.

An ideal American Cocker Spaniel

Note — 1. Height is determined by a line perpendicular to the ground from the top of the shoulder-blades, the dog standing naturally with its forelegs and the lower hind legs parallel to the line of the measurement. 2. Male animals should have two apparently normal testicles fully descended into the scrotum.

Who said you could not have too much of a good thing? I am all in favour of full Standards but I think the Standard of the American Cocker goes a little too far. The judge is supposed to award prizes but I reckon the judge who knows and fully comprehends the American Cocker Standard deserves a prize himself.

The Standard sets itself out to describe a working dog and almost insists that this is a more important aspect than showing off in a beauty ring. Why then is there such detailed note of colour and variations of colour? Would a Field dog be penalized with the colour markings that are penalized in the Standard?

I also get the impression that coat is really not all that important when it talks about medium length on the body and faults 'excessive' coat — but the whole preparation of the American Cocker for the show ring demands as much coat as possible for the exhibitor to cut and shape. This is not meant as a criticism of the exhibitor, but as a criticism of the Standard which just does not admit to the common practice going on in the show ring.

The differences between the English and American Cocker Spaniel Standards are fascinating and one could write a book comparing the two.

I said earlier that Breed Standards do matter, and I stick by that, but in practice it is a fact that we each read what we want in a Breed Standard. There is no other way of explaining varying show results when the same dogs meet each other in competition and yet very often awards are not consistent.

Buying a Puppy

Buying a puppy can be one of the most exciting things you ever do. To think that a tiny puppy will grow, hopefully, into a beautiful loving companion, anxious to please you, and being completely satisfied with a pat on the head for a reward, is really quite something. That puppy will never hate you if you treat it properly and kindly. It is really only capable of affection towards you.

But selecting a puppy does have its problems. Puppies change. You must have heard stories of the runt of the litter turning into a Champion, or the best in a litter never developing into anything of consequence.

There are some guidelines — never buy a Cocker from a pet shop or kennel dealing in a number of different breeds — always buy a Cocker from a breeder of Cockers. You will probably not have to pay any more for it, but the breeder gives you a back up of experience to help you with any difficulties that may arise. A dealing kennel or a pet shop usually does not want to know if there are any problems after the sale.

Cockers are such a popular breed that you should have little difficulty in finding a reliable breeder living within ten or twenty miles, and if you write to The Kennel Club you will be sent the name and address of a local breeder. The dog papers have advertisements of puppies available and this will give you a choice of kennels.

Always buy a puppy outright. Do not pay a deposit and regular payments over a period of time. If you cannot afford to buy a Cocker puppy outright you should not have one because you cannot afford to innoculate it and feed it properly. Never buy a Cocker on 'Breeding Terms'. This means paying a small amount originally but agreeing to let the breeder have puppies back from any litters a bitch might have. This is messy and you cannot get out of a breeding agreement easily if you change your mind.

The ideal age for buying a puppy is eight to twelve weeks of age. By this time the puppy should have been fully weaned and will co-operate with efforts to house train and even lead training — though this can wait for another month. Sometimes you get a better buy by purchasing an older puppy. I never sell puppies around Christmas time and if I am presented with a litter at this time I wait until mid-January before I am willing to sell and this means the puppy may be older than twelve weeks. An older puppy may be more set in its ways, but you have the advantage that it is more developed in its rearing.

Before actually buying a puppy prepare for its arrival. A dog basket or box must be bought — remember though a wicker basket can be chewed, so a fibreglass sleeping box might be an investment. Get food in for the puppy — eggs, milk, Farex, good quality tinned dog meat and a box of high quality puppy biscuit meal. Make sure your garden is adequately fenced. Generally Cockers do not run off at every opportunity but care should be taken to ensure that the exercise area for the puppy is escape-proof. Buy a collar and lead, but remember your puppy is very small so the collar must be adjustable. Explain to the pet shop owner that the collar and lead are for a puppy. Mineral and vitamin tablets can be bought later but a feeding bowl and drinking bowl must be bought in advance of the puppy's arrival.

When you visit a kennel that has puppies for sale make a proper appointment and be on time. Do not go to a kennel wearing your best clothes. The breeder may allow you to mix with the dogs and they may welcome you with muddy paws. The breeder will not think a great deal of you if you push aside a show of affection because you are more concerned about your clothing.

Go armed with plenty of questions. Has the puppy been wormed? It is house-trained? Has it done well in its rearing? How long has it been fully weaned? Is it fussy over its food? Is it having any special vitamin or mineral supplements? A breeder is only too pleased to answer questions and welcomes the questioning.

Temperament is the all-important thing. When all the finer breed points have been forgotten you still have to live with the dog and a good temperament is essential. It is useful to see the puppies' parents if they are both at the kennel. You must see the mother of the puppies and if you like her, and the sire, the chances are you will like the puppy. If you do not like the parents; if they are bad tempered; if they are really not very good specimens of the breed, you will not like a puppy from the litter. Once you have made up your mind to have a Cocker be prepared to buy the puppy there and then if you like it. Do not go from kennel to kennel and be lost in choice and do not expect a breeder to reserve a puppy for you because you are not sure whether you like it. The chances are someone else will snap it up and you have lost the opportunity of buying that puppy. On the other hand, do not buy a puppy merely because at some inconvenience to yourself you have travelled some distance to see it, or because you are pressured by the breeder into buying a puppy. You must like the look of the puppy otherwise do not buy — it is as simple as that.

Luckily the Cocker puppy does look rather like a miniature Cocker Spaniel, though the featherings on the legs will not have fully developed. That might sound like a strange statement to make about a puppy but you would be surprised at the number of puppies of different breeds that look nothing like the mature dog. Some of the puppies of larger coated breeds bear little resemblance to the finished product.

Look for an alert puppy with a good glossy coat. Check the eyes and nose for any discharge. The ears should start level with the eye-line and should be the length of the tip of the nose. Examine inside the ears for cleanliness. Avoid a thin puppy which may be a poor doer. Check the mouth for the bite of the teeth. Do not have a pup which is undershot; that is, the lower teeth are in front of the upper teeth. This can alter but it is rare to do so. A Cocker puppy should always be lively and have no fear. If a puppy has a prominent fault the honest breeder will point it out instantly and it should have some effect on the price. If you want a puppy as a pet you are not so interested in the finer breed points, but you still want a healthy, bold, sound puppy and any sign of nervousness should be avoided at any price.

Be suspicious of excessive scratching. It is not uncommon for a dog to have an occasional flea but a breeder should constantly check his stock for parasites and you would hope not to find one on a puppy offered for sale.

The puppy should be square in outline and the tail should be set on just below the level of the topline. Cocker puppies do tend to sometimes carry their tails a little high so this is difficult to assess always, but as long as the set of the tail is correct the tail should eventually be carried properly.

Make sure the puppy has no sores on his body and that he is not limping. Ask the breeder particularly whether the puppy has been wormed and when it should be wormed again. Worms are the very devil and affect the puppy's growth and condition quite severely but they are easily got rid of with tablets from the vet.

Puppies do vary and it is impossible to accurately and specifically describe the size, height and weight of a puppy. You have to choose by instinct — you might be right, or you could be wrong. The head is difficult to assess in the young Cocker puppy, and coat length and quality is also difficult to assess. That is why it is so important to see the parents, as they give you a good idea of how your puppy will eventually turn out.

Particularly ask how the puppy has been fed and ask for a diet sheet giving details of feeding, amounts, the type of food and regularity of meals.

Once you have paid for your puppy you need a number of documents: the pedigree; The Kennel Club Registration Card; signed Transfer Form and diet sheet. If you pay cash for your puppy you should expect to receive all these documents when you take your puppy away. If you pay by cheque it is reasonable to expect the breeder to post the documents on to you when the cheque has been cleared.

On the journey home it is quite possible the puppy will be sick — it may be his first journey in a car, so take some newspapers and be prepared. When you get home allow an hour or so before you attempt to offer any food or milk, though a bowl of water should be handy because exploring a new home can be thirsty work for a Cocker puppy. You should already have the basket or box ready for your puppy and make sure it is not in a draughty place. If you have an old jumper or woolly garment put that in the sleeping box, because now the puppy will know you a little and on that first night

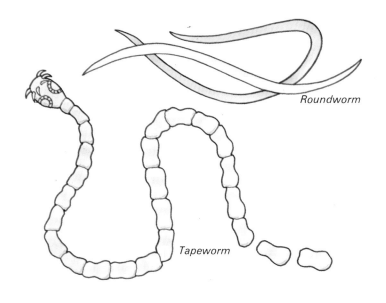
Roundworm

Tapeworm

Adult flea

Biting louse

Engorged female tick

Mite (microscopic)

Sucking louse

Parasites

33

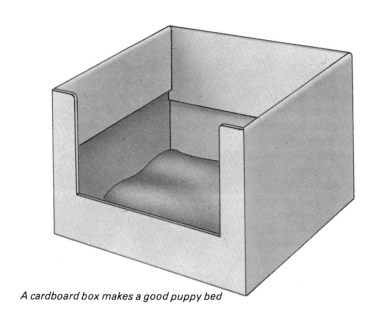

A cardboard box makes a good puppy bed

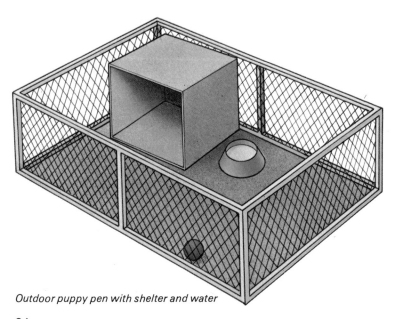

Outdoor puppy pen with shelter and water

in a new home it might help him to settle down better.

Play with your puppy before you retire for the night and tire him out. Do not allow him to sleep before you go to bed because sure as anything he will wake up in the middle of the night and howl the place down. A bowl of warm milk will help pacify him — never use pills or drugs to get a puppy to go to sleep.

You may be lucky with that first night and have a peaceful time, but be prepared to get up and see to the puppy if he does suddenly wake up and wonder where on earth he his. Remember, until now he has spent his life with his mother and brothers and sisters, and he has known every inch of his terrain. Now he is out in the big wide world and he may be very puzzled as to where he is and what has happened. Never take a puppy to bed with you unless you want a dog at the foot of the bed for the rest of its life.

When you get up next morning be prepared for at the least a puddle — maybe something worse and much more messy! This is where you start your house-training. Put paper down as near the outside door as possible and everytime you give the puppy a meal, or every hour, or whenever you remember, put the puppy outside in the garden and wait with him until he does his toilet. When he has done it show him you are pleased with his perfor-mance and say a kindly word. A puppy will almost certainly evacuate his bowels soon after he has had a large meal, and he will empty his bladder after he has had a drink. Be prepared, and you will soon have your puppy house-trained.

Give your puppy a name. This is important and the sooner a name is used the sooner the puppy will do the things you want it to. The name might be associated with his registered name, but these are sometimes very grand sounding but not practical in use. Use the puppy's name often and get him used to it. It might be a good idea after the first night to telephone the breeder just to say everything is all right, or to ask any questions you had forgotten.

If you have bought your puppy as a pet you will forgive its development if it loses out on a lot of Breed Standard points, but is loving and happy. If you bought the puppy with the intention of showing it, the breeder should be honest with you and tell you its show potential in his or her opinion. It is of little benefit to a breeder to have sub-standard stock carrying his or her name shown in the ring.

One of the most important things to happen to your puppy is his innoculation. At twelve weeks of age he must be protected against distemper. Ignore anything you may read about hygiene being effective against distemper — it is not. If the distemper virus is in your area your dog will die without the proper protection of a simple innoculation. Book your puppy into the vet's surgery as soon as you get it home.

You have to be prepared for the most promising puppy to turn out a dud. If they all turned out to be Champions there would be little point in going into a show ring — it would all be done by computer, based on pedigree, price and breeder's rating.

You have bought a Cocker puppy. Be content with it — make it happy and it will repay in love and affection that cannot ever be price-tagged.

Cocker Spaniel puppies

Care of your Cocker

A young Cocker requires nourishing food. Table scraps are not sufficient to keep a youngster in good condition. From six to twelve months one meal a day should be of raw meat. Another meal can be a milky feed, and another a mixture of biscuit meal and good quality tinned dog food. You will usually find that the cost of dog food, and canned food particularly, is commensurate with the quality. Do not feed a growing youngster on cheap food; you will regret it later. From twelve months onwards two meals a day should be sufficient to keep your Cocker in good condition and health. Fresh clean water should always be available, and one meal might be broken dog biscuits, the other raw or lightly cooked meat, or good quality tinned food. At one time tinned dog food was regarded with some disdain by some breeders, but the quality of branded tinned dog food has improved immensely in the last few years, and while some claims of some tinned dog food must be taken with the proverbial pinch of salt, generally they are of nutritional value and, of course, are very convenient.

However, like humans, the dog likes a variety of food and the occasional meal of tripe or sheep's paunch will go down very well, as will fish (very carefully boned) and sheep's heads, but you will often find a change of diet, though welcome, will sometimes make the dog's motions loose. This will not harm the dog as long as the condition does not continue for any length of time.

Always be careful of bones. While admitting that in the wild the dog would eat bones, they can cause a multitude of problems. Even the marrow bone (which a dog loves) can cause damage if chips of bone are swallowed. Chicken bones must never be given to a dog. A dog's stomach has gastric juices that are capable of digesting almost everything the dog can swallow, but there is always the danger of sharp bones tearing the intestines. So bones, sadly, are out.

In place of giving your dog bones, which are very good for the teeth, try a hard dog biscuit, which can virtually do the same job.

It is almost impossible to detail accurately the amount of food your dog will eat. Cockers are generally good eaters and will probably eat ten to twenty per cent more food than they actually require to keep fit. Each dog is an individual when it comes to the amount of food consumed — just like humans. Your dog will soon let you know how much food he needs. After a meal it is important to take up uneaten food. It gets stale very quickly, attracts flies, and if you leave food down, one meal starts drifting into the next meal.

We have already discussed house-training in the puppy section of this book and training is mentioned in a little more detail in the chapter on dog shows and Field Trials, but an additional word here about training. Get your dog used to being called by name. Use simple words of command like 'sit!' and gently press the youngster down into the sit position, rewarding him when he does it properly.

Training a Cocker Spaniel to sit

From four months of age start to lead train your puppy and get him used to wearing a collar with your name and address printed on it. This is a legal requirement in most cities. When you put a lead on him let him play with it before demonstrating to him that the lead is your way of restraining and restricting his movement, guiding him along the route *you* want to go. All training must be done gently and without strong discipline. If you break a dog's spirit at this stage of development you will have an unhappy cringing dog that is no pleasure to own at all.

Plenty of exercise is needed, lead training is essential and the Cocker must be trained on the lead to walk without straining or pulling — a loose lead is desirable. Straining and pulling, some breeders believe, is responsible for creating an unsound front and shoulders. Slack or open feet can be improved by plenty of walking or running on a hard surface — it helps to tighten up feet considerably. Playing and running freely is helpful to develop muscle and body condition.

Even if you never take your dog to dog shows, Field Trials or Obedience Tests, it is as well to get a good degree of obedience so that you both live happily with each other. An obedient dog is a joy to own — a disobedient one is a pleasure to no one.

Your Cocker has certain natural instincts, such as retrieving; develop these in play to your enjoyment and the dog's happiness.

Hygiene is very important with a young Cocker. If he comes in with muddy paws, wipe them down. If he has been in a field, check his paws and coat for any burrs or grass seeds. Grass seeds particularly can be a great nuisance to a dog and, if they work their way under the skin, can cause pain and discomfort and can lead to abscesses.

Never let your dog lick pools of dirty water, but if he wants to eat green grass then let him — he will probably vomit soon after and this removes from his stomach excess bile and any fur that has accumulated.

Wash your Cocker's basket or sleeping box daily with a fairly strong disinfectant. You really cannot be too careful about hygiene. A Cocker is quite naturally a hardy dog able to fend off disease, but you can help by ensuring that his feeding and drinking bowls are thoroughly clean at all times and that he is never kept dirty for long.

If you have just one Cocker you will probably want to keep him in the house and he does make an excellent house pet, but it is also a good idea to let him have a kennel outside in the yard or garden. A place of his own where he can rest, if he wants to, or just go to when you humans become a little to tiresome — a daytime sanctuary if you like. The kennel needs to be a good size to accommodate him in comfort. It needs to be at least twice his height from toe to the top of his head, and half as long again as his body from nose to tail in width and length. A bed of straw in the kennel makes a comfortable resting place but the straw must be changed once a week. Never put clothes or sacking in the outside kennel as these can harbour unwanted parasites. Make sure the outside kennel if draught-free.

Never chain your dog up for long periods — if you have to restrain him in this way make sure he has a good length of chain to move about on. I hate to see a dog chained up — it is most unnatural, and can be depressing for the dog. I always feel that a dog kept on the end of a chain is in a home where the people really have not the time to spend with him. Those people, to my thinking, should not own a dog.

Grooming is an important aspect of owning a Cocker and if you cannot spare at least ten minutes a day to groom your dog you should perhaps think of having another breed. A well-groomed dog rarely has fleas and lice and a good brushing and combing every day will keep the coat in good condition. Brush the dog all over — head, ears, body and legs, but gently. The ears need grooming lightly inside and out, but never probe the ears with a sharp object as this can be very dangerous. Use the brush well on the body then comb through. Take care with the ears, otherwise you will take out too much feathering. If you groom daily you will hardly need to trim your dog because you will remove dead coat with the brush and comb. Do not let your Cocker go for days without grooming — he can get to look very scruffy, feel uncomfortable and lose coat condition very quickly. You will find that once he is used to being groomed he will look forward to it and even demand it. After all, he is getting all your attention and he thrives on that!

Trimming a Cocker for the show ring is not something that can be taught with a few paragraphs in a book such as this. It takes quite a lot of experience before you can trim successfully for the show ring and you can only learn by experience and watching others. The finger-and-thumb method of trimming has been used for nearly a hundred years and, properly done, it is the best method. Never cut the hair with scissors because when it grows in again the coat will go curly. This would be improper in the show ring and looks unsightly even for a pet Cocker. The only place where cutting with scissors is necessary is around the feet and between the toes, but very carefully.

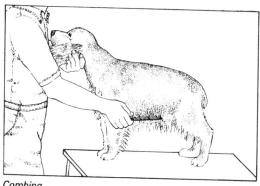

Combing

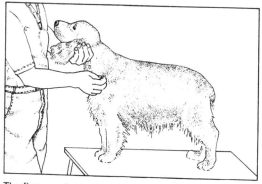

The finger and thumb method

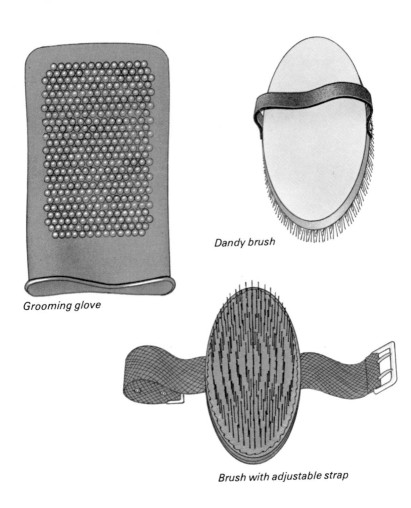

Grooming glove

Dandy brush

Brush with adjustable strap

Oval bristle brush

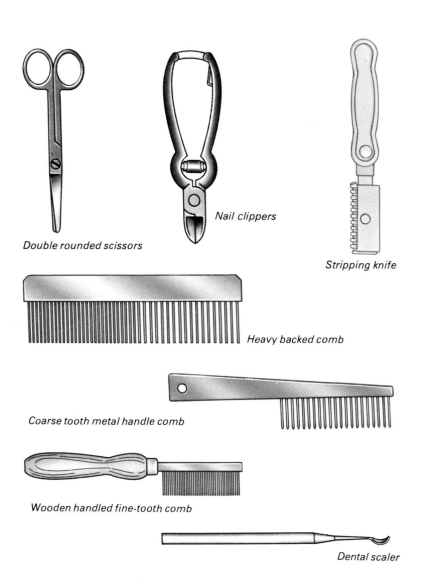

Double rounded scissors

Nail clippers

Stripping knife

Heavy backed comb

Coarse tooth metal handle comb

Wooden handled fine-tooth comb

Dental scaler

There are many useful items that can be purchased for grooming the particular coat type that you own

Good presentation enhances the breed points. It has to be admitted that many Cockers seen in the show ring are scissored, but this is improper and your true Cocker breeder will tell you so. If your Cocker is sent to a dog beauty parlour the chances are they will use scissors and clippers, but the *proper* way to prepare a Cocker is by finger and thumb. The dog beauty parlour just could not do this — they probably have not got the experience and the time it takes would be uneconomic for them. It takes a period of weeks to prepare the Cocker for the show ring. A little trim each day will make the whole thing less laborious. Thumb and finger, together with brush and comb (a number six comb) and no fancy lotions are really needed. The natural oils in the coat promoted by good grooming should be sufficient to give your Cocker a gleaming finish. Remember, the coat and the featherings of the Cocker are two of their loveliest attractions.

In the show world you cannot ignore daily grooming, and then have a mad rush the day before a show bathing and grooming furiously in the hope all will be well. Grooming a Cocker is a necessary daily routine and if you have not the time perhaps you ought to keep tortoises.

American Cockers are a different thing altogether. The American is trimmed on the head, the top part of the ears and a deep body saddle is also clipped out. Scissors are used as well to thin coat where necessary. It was probably all this preparation and clipping that upset established English Cocker breeders when the American first came over to Britain. It surprised many dog people in other breeds to see Cocker exhibitors happily clipping away at their Americans in a way that would have been forbidden and abhorrent on their own English Cockers.

There has been quite a lot of controversy about the presentation in the show ring of English Cockers and in 1963 a very famous British judge, Mr. Leo C. Wilson took to task Cocker exhibitors for trimming and shaving the necks of their dogs. At the time it was obviously happening but it took a judge of Mr. Wilson's status to bring it all out into the open. The matter was taken up by the famous American judge, Mrs. C. Bede Maxwell, who said that improper presentation in the show ring was happening world-wide.

The safety razor has been used in trimming Cockers. It may be less harsh than scissors and the coat may not grow wavy, but strictly speaking it is still improper. The feathering of the Cocker is important — not only does it look attractive but it has the practical use of protecting the dog in its work. The whole art of trimming with finger and thumb is to improve the outline and appearance of the dog in accordance with the Standard of points, while at the same time preserving its naturalness.

A Cocker completely stripped of hair on its neck may on first glance appear to have a longer neck than if it had a natural coat, but it looks less like a proper Cocker. Cocker breeders like to keep the breed looking like a working dog even if not all of them are given an opportunity of working.

It has to be said that some judges are taken in by scissoring, shaving and trimming, and at smaller shows you might get away with it, but at Championship Shows you could be sent out of the show ring for improper preparation.

How often you should bath your Cocker is a difficult question to answer. Not too often, as bathing removes the natural oils from the coat and this is a particular problem with show dogs that are bathed frequently. Bathing once a week would be detrimental to the dog's general condition. Once every two months would be better but, of course, if your Cocker gets very dirty after an outing, since you do not want to have a smelly dirty dog in the house, it might be a signal for a bath. There are some very good dry shampoos on the market and available at pet shops, and talcum powder rubbed into the coat and brushed out leaves a pleasant scent, but it is important to brush and comb the talcum powder out of the coat and feathering as it can coagulate into lumps that turn into matts.

Sometimes the feathering of a Cocker gets very matted, especially where the owner has been a little careless over regular grooming. After a bath it might help to put on a cream rinse conditioner for normal hair, and then comb out with this on while still wet. It will leave the coat silky and soft.

Bathing a Cocker is fairly simple with just commonsense rules to follow. Wet the dog through with warm water — not too cold and not too hot — shampoo thoroughly, being very careful of the eyes and inside the ears, and rinse thoroughly. There are a number of excellent dog shampoos available but I like using Coconut Oil shampoo as it does seem to put a little oil back into the dog's coat. Drying can be done by briskly rubbing with a towel in front of a fire, and then brushing and combing through using at the same time a hand-held hair drier. It is a good idea to get a young dog used to this treatment because if you suddenly introduce a hair blower/drier, the dog can be quite upset by the noise.

Always be very careful to keep the newly bathed dog out of draughts, and in cold weather never let him go outside until he is properly and fully dry. It is very easy for a dog to catch a cold or chill and this can be avoided with a little care.

As a dog gets older body smells get stronger and great care should be taken bathing an old dog. It is best to avoid bathing in cold weather altogether.

No chapter on the care of the Cocker Spaniel would be complete without special mention of the care of ears. Not every Cocker breeder will admit it but Cockers' ears can get very smelly. In some kennels the breeder is so used to the smell that he does not notice it, but visitors do. At least once a week the inside of the ear should be cleaned out with a piece of cotton wool. Boracic powder can be used, or you can ask your vet to make up a cleaning solution that will contain a mild antiseptic. The old Cocker particularly needs careful attention to his ears as the smell can be much stronger in old age and is offensive to other people and, I suspect, irritating to the dog. The problem is that the shape and length of the Cocker's ear does not allow fresh air to circulate and if you let trouble develop in the ear it can cause all kinds of problems, such as canker or an infectious discharge. Regular attention to ears is very important and, again, if you feel you have not the time for this, perhaps the Cocker is not the dog for you.

Do be careful in hot weather with your Cocker. The water bowl should be changed more often and kept scrupulously clean. The dog should not lay out in the direct sun for hours on end; try and make sure there is shade in the garden in which he can lie. If your Cocker is affected by the heat, a cold wet flannel at the back of the head and neck will assist him to get over his distress, but a severe case of heatstroke may need veterinary attention. Again this is one of those things that can be avoided by a little care and attention.

A word here about your Cocker when he gets old. Just as humans age, so does the dog, but a little extra care will ensure your dog enjoys his old age.

Grooming daily is still important but be a little more gentle. Bathing, as I have already said, should never be done in cold weather unless really necessary. Attention to ears is needed a little more closely in the old dog, and instead of feeding one meal a day, which is really all the adult dog needs, the old dog might benefit by having two smaller meals a day. The older dog still needs exercising but never force him to walk further than he wants to go. Feeding is no problem but cut the food up into smaller portions — as a young or adult dog your Cocker may have enjoyed largish lumps of meat to tackle and chew. As he gets older he may lose some teeth and chewing may be difficult. You may read some reference books that say dogs do not chew their food but swallow in greedily and the gastric juices take care of the food and break it down for digestion. This is true, but I have known many dogs chew their food and enjoy it in the same way as we do. There is some very good tinned food specially made for the old dog which is more easily digested and this is to be recommended on the advice of your vet.

The day comes when your dog dies. There is little written about this but, just as we humans have to die, eventually a dog does the same. I am a firm believer in dogs dying with dignity. If you think this sounds a little strange let me explain. As your dog gets old he may need continual veterinary treatment once something is diagnosed, such as failing kidneys, liver problems or a heart condition. Dogs can live with all these ailments more happily than us humans, and they can all be treated, but I do advise that you do not make unnecessary visits to the vet. I do not like to see an elderly ailing dog poked, prodded and injected unnecessarily.

When should we put a dog down? Never I hope. Personally I would not put a dog to sleep unless he was in pain. If there is something physically wrong but the dog is not distressed by it, I would leave it alone. I have known blind and deaf dogs living very happily with families who cared a great deal and gave affection to their dog. But the day may come when the decision has to be made to put your dog finally to sleep. It can only be your decision — you cannot expect anyone else to decide — you may take veterinary advice or the advice of someone with experience with dogs, but in the end *you* have to make up your own mind. When you do, take my advice and be with your dog at the end. How awful just to leave your dog with the vet and have strangers with it at the end. This is unfair to the dog. He has earned his right by a lifetime of companionship to have you comforting him at the end. It may not be pleasant for you, but it is the right thing to do if you think about it.

However, let us end this chapter on the care of your Cocker on a cheerful note. A Cocker is a long-living dog and ten years of age may not be old for some Cockers. They often live for fourteen or fifteen years. So you have many years of happiness and a unique friendship ahead of you with your Cocker.

Breeding

It is exciting breeding a litter of puppies — planning the litter; whelping and rearing the puppies; seeing them develop and grow up; and placing them in good and loving homes, is rewarding — *but* before a litter is planned you should ask yourself why you are considering breeding, and you must be prepared for the drawbacks as well as the pleasures.

Why breed at all? If your object is to make money out of a litter, think again. That really is not a good enough reason. Cocker puppies do sell quite easily but money should not be the first consideration, and if you have a certain amount of bad luck you could find yourself losing financially. If your bitch needs attention during pregnancy the vet has to be paid. The puppies need attention anyway, docking of tails, etc., and that costs money. If the bitch needs any assistance at the birth it could be at an unsociable time (in the middle of the night) and the vet will not turn out without payment. So if money is your first concern do not breed dogs. Go and breed Arabian horses or mink! There is no room in the dog world for money-making breeders!

Is your bitch good enough to breed from? It is a question you should seriously ask yourself. If her temperament is not first-class perhaps it might be wiser not to breed from her. Experts nearly all agree that the temperament of the bitch has a lot to do with the temperament of her puppies.

Puppies seem so friendly and playful; you would not think they could be bad tempered, but I can tell you I was once attacked quite viciously by a litter of seven week old puppies which the owner asked me to look at. As soon as I approached them they went for me, snarling and snapping. It may have been fear but it really does not matter — the chances of those puppies growing up good tempered and well-mannered is remote. Needless to say, the mother was a bad tempered bitch from which breeding should never have been attempted.

For me, temperament is the number one priority in breeding. Other breeders may be more concerned with breed points but many of these points can be assisted by the choice of a good and suitable mate. Faults can sometimes be rectified at the first attempt of breeding. Also it has to be admitted that, just to confound the experts who proudly match up a dog and bitch, faults very often do not reproduce themselves.

If you have a bitch and you decide to breed from her, where do you start? First, make sure your bitch is healthy, and this is something you cannot attain just at the time she is ready to breed. Good health is something you must have at all times. Overweight is perhaps the most unhealthy aspect of a bitch which will certainly affect breeding. A cocker must be well-exercised, sensibly fed and properly groomed. These simple requirements will ensure good health and assist with a successful breeding programme.

Selecting a suitable stud-dog can be a big problem. Too many stud-dog owners can see no fault in their dog; they are blind to its unsuitability for breeding. So asking the dog's owner if it is right for your bitch is often of no use at all. *You* have to decide, but you might be assisted with advice from the breeder who sold you your bitch. If the breeder is sensible you will get help selecting a suitable stud, and you might get assistance with the dogs to avoid by way of unsuitable breeding, incorrect temperament, or incompatible pedigree.

It might be helpful to see a stud-dog's progeny in the show ring. The only problem here is that you do not know what the dam was like. Whatever you do be prepared to travel some distance for a suitable dog. Breedng to the dog next door or conveniently round the corner will be difficult to explain to the prospective puppy buyer who asks why you chose that particular dog.

If you like a dog's progeny have a good look at the dog. Make sure you like the look of him. Look for a merry Cocker — one of the best phrases to describe the breed. Search for a healthy looking dog of good temperament, then ask the owner for a pedigree and compare it with the pedigree of your bitch. If the same breeding lines appear in both pedigrees ask knowledgeable Cocker folk about those breeding lines — the faults and the virtues. If the same dog appears in both pedigrees ask around just how good was that ancestor.

Unfortunately just after the Second World War, when Cockers were very popular, some very poor breeding occurred with little thought of pedigrees, but you might be fortunate in getting a coherent five generation pedigree with the stud-dog you are considering.

A knowledgeable breeder can read a lot in this pedigree and if you are fortunate to know one, he or she could be very helpful in advising you of the suitability of the stud-dog.

There are all sorts of stories that stud-dogs are dominant in their progeny. It is not the case in my experience. Puppies take on the characteristics of both parents though they *may* favour one or the other. You certainly owe it to yourself, the prospective puppy owner, and the breed, to try and select a good and suitable dog for your bitch. It is not something to be decided upon quickly — though you should have a stud-dog in mind well before your bitch is ready for mating.

Avoid a shy or nervous stud-dog. These characteristics are undesirable and almost certainly will pass on to the puppies. As I have said before, breed faults are the very devil to sort out. I have known stud-dogs with poor angulated rear quarters, sire puppies that are well-angulated. Of all the points most likely to reproduce themselves in puppies, poor heads seem to dominate. If you choose a dog with a thick coarse head, you are very likely to get similarly-headed puppies, but the exception proves the rule, and I have known parents with coarse heads produce fine-headed puppies. Nature has no absolute set pattern on breed point reproduction.

I can honestly say that whenever I have bred a litter there has been a purpose behind the breeding. I mated a certain dog with a certain bitch for a reason. I have to admit that the pairing has not always produced the progeny I aimed for — nature has a habit of upsetting the highest ideals — but when a prospective puppy buyer looks at my puppies I can explain what I have aimed for. I can get the dog and bitch together and point out breed points and characteristics I was anxious to maintain. I would suggest it is sensible for you to do the same.

After satisfying yourself that your bitch is suitable for breeding, satisfy yourself that the chosen mate equally has points that you would like to see in the puppies you hope to breed.

If this is your first litter try to find an experienced stud-dog and make sure you take your bitch to him when the time is right for the mating. Your bitch is likely to come into 'use' or come into 'season' any time from six to eight months, but you must not mate her at this first season. She is not fully mature physically or mentally and, although she could have a litter at a very early age, it would be unfair to expose her to stresses in this way. Her second or even third season is the one to aim for. The tell-tale signs are enlarging of the vulva and constant licking. The first day proper of the season is when blood is seen round the vulva. Count ten days from this time and she is ready for mating. Immediately your bitch comes into season inform the owner of the chosen stud-dog and book for the tenth day, with a repeat mating on the twelfth day if possible. A second mating two days after the first is always desirable, in my view, but it is not essential.

Before the mating make proper arrangements about paying for the stud service. Most breeders will take a fee which is usually about half the price of a good puppy, but owners of stud-dogs can charge whatever they like. No governing body lays down the price of stud fees or the cost of a puppy. You will pay more for a Champion than you would for a pet dog. The chances are that the Champion will provide better quality puppies but this is not always the case and many Champions themselves have parents that could be classed as pet dogs.

I always advise the payment of a stud fee rather than allowing the owner of the stud-dog to take a puppy instead of a stud fee. The latter method of payment is messy and allows the dog owner to take the best puppy in the litter. If you can afford it, pay a proper stud fee. If you cannot afford it perhaps you should not be breeding with your bitch anyway, because you will certainly have to pay out for some veterinary service.

Some years ago it was common practice for bitches to be sent in a box by train to a stud-dog. This is thoroughly undesirable and puts a bitch under stress at the very time she should be happy, content and relaxed. Travel with your bitch to the stud-dog and if the dog is experienced trust the owner to effect the mating. If you are present at the mating do not be too upset if your bitch does not seem to be a very willing partner. She may have been flirting with everything on four legs during her season but, at the last and most important minute, she may change her mind. Well, hard lines! The job has got to be done and whoever is effecting the mating has to be firm with the bitch — and the dog, if necessary. The bitch may be held firmly with the muzzle held in one hand. The dog will mount the bitch and if he is experienced he should need no further assistance. The bitch may yelp when the dog has entered her and a 'tie' may occur. The end of the dog's penis swells and he is held in position and unable to withdraw. Usually, to make both dog and bitch comfortable, one of the dog's back legs is turned over the bitch and they are in the back to back position. This tie may last anything from five minutes to an hour. The actual time of the tie is of no consequence and sometimes there is no tie at all but the bitch may still become pregnant. As soon as the dog and bitch have parted, separate them completely and keep the bitch calm.

Before the mating make sure the bitch empties herself and after the mating allow at least an hour before the bitch again does her toilet.

Pregnancy lasts sixty-three days, but there can be two or three days difference either way. During pregnancy your bitch needs good nutritional food and, after about three weeks, some additional nourishment; an egg a day mixed with warm milk is beneficial, and some multi-vitamin tablets such as 'Canovel' are useful additives. Do not overfeed your bitch during pregnancy, but if she wants a little more food than usual, then let her have it.

The first sign of a successful mating is usually the swelling of the teats and perhaps after three weeks the swelling of her tummy. After five or six weeks puppies can sometimes be seen moving around her tummy area when she is lying down.

Towards the end of her pregnancy the bitch may get easily tired and want more rest. Exercise is still important but respect your bitch's desire for less activity.

As I have said, it is quite common for a bitch to whelp two or three days before or after the conventional sixty-three days. I have known a bitch go a full week over the period, but if your bitch does go a week over and it is obvious that she has got puppies it might be a good idea to visit the vet. There is no need to panic — there may be nothing wrong at all — but your vet is the best judge.

If there is no sign of puppies and it is obvious that the mating was unsuccessful, in fairness to yourself and the owner of the dog, at the full time of sixty-three days ask the vet to examine your bitch and give you a certificate that she is not in whelp. Send a copy of this certificate to the owner of the stud-dog with a *request* for a repeat mating. Usually owners of stud-dogs will allow a repeat mating at no extra charge if a bitch misses, but this is a concession and not a firm rule. You pay for the services of a stud-dog for the mating — if no puppies result you could not possibly apportion the blame properly. It could be the stud-dog's fault — but it could equally be the bitch's fault. No one will ever know. A veterinary certificate puts the matter properly in black and white and, as I say, a request for a repeat mating will usually be granted.

The great moment comes for the birth of the puppies. At least a week before they are due the whelping box should be available for your bitch. For a Cocker a good and comfortably sized whelping box should be 40in (100cm) by 24in (60cm) — this will adequately contain the puppies when they get active. Get your bitch used to sleeping in the whelping box at least a week before the puppies are due.

The first sign that the whelping is imminent is that your bitch will become very restless, scratching around in her whelping box and perhaps crying a little and panting. She will start contractions and bearing down, and this means the puppies can start arriving any time from five minutes to an hour. A Cocker rarely needs assistance at whelping, but if your bitch is bearing down strongly for more than an hour it might be worthwhile to call the vet for assistance. In any case a few days before the puppies are due it is useful to warn him that you have a litter on the way and book him to see the bitch after she has had her puppies.

The chances are that the first puppy will be born fit and well. The normal delivery is head first but puppies can be born feet first, tail first or even back first. They are covered in a bag or membrane and they are attached to their mother with a cord — the umbilical cord. The bitch will usually need no assistance to bite through this cord and lick life into her puppy.

There is sometimes a great mass of afterbirth and it is just as well to let the bitch eat this unless she shoves it away. The bitch instinctively knows that an afterbirth is attached to her puppy and if you take it away before she has a good sniff she may get distressed looking for it. It sounds revolting that the bitch should eat the afterbirth but it is perfectly natural and reverts back to the wild when the bitch realized that any smelly meat would attract unwanted visitors and predators. It is also said to contain nourishment for the bitch.

Cocker Spaniel bitch with her litter

By the time of the next puppy's arrival, which is usually somewhat easier than the first, the first-born puppy will already be at its mother's teat and sucking contentedly. Puppies can arrive every ten minutes or every hour. If the bitch seems a little distressed and it is some time since a puppy was born it does no harm to take her outside to relieve herself, but watch her carefully in case she expels a puppy, which I have known to happen. Do not keep her away from the whelping box for any length of time, as she desperately wants to get back to the puppies she has had.

A little warm milk in a bowl is often acceptable in between giving birth to puppies, but do not try and feed her at this time.

There is no set number of puppies in a litter. Your bitch may have just one puppy or she may have ten, but when she has apparently finished the whelping get her to stand up and gently feel her tummy to see if any more puppies are left. They will feel like hard lumps inside her, but be gentle.

The following day ask the vet to call and inspect the bitch and puppies, and perhaps give the bitch an antibiotic injection as a precaution against infection.

Cocker Spaniel puppies feeding

Of course, the vet should be called during the whelping if the bitch gets into extreme difficulty, but do not fuss too much. Bitches have been having puppies naturally for centuries without your help! If you are too fussy you will upset your bitch needlessly.

Keep the puppies warm and out of draughts. The heated fibre-glass bed makes an ideal nesting box — warming from underneath and allowing fresh air to circulate in the box, as opposed to an infra-red lamp hovering above the box which can sometimes distress the bitch because of its intensity.

How many puppies should the bitch rear? This is an awkward question to answer. If your bitch has ten or twelve puppies it is obvious it will be a strain for her to rear all of these — but which puppies to choose? Well check the puppies thoroughly for any deformities; these are rare but if you have a deformity now is the time to remove it. Unwanted puppies should always be destroyed by a vet — humanely, quickly and painlessly. If a choice of puppies has to be made the smaller puppies should go first, but it is a problem — are you destroying a possible Champion? If a selection of puppies has to be made try and get the advice of an experienced breeder.

The Cocker puppy's tail has to be docked between four and six days of age unless the litter is premature and the puppies are not properly developed. I do not propose to go into great detail here about docking. It *must* be done by an experienced Cocker breeder or a vet. You must not dock a tail without knowing precisely what you are doing. About a third of the tail is left on. At the same time the dew-claws need removing. These are rather like thumbs on the front and, occasionally, back legs. Again this is a job for the vet or an experienced breeder. Wrongly done the puppy can bleed to death — I must be blunt about it. Dew-claw removal and tail-docking is not something the novice breeder can do and a litter of puppies can be ruined by improper docking. Never use a rubber band to dock the tail; I have seen this done and I consider it very cruel.

Some vets are not at all happy about docking tails and consider this to be cosmetic mutilation and you may have difficulty in getting a vet to do the operation. At the present time the Cocker's tail must be docked to enter the show ring as a proper specimen of the breed. If this is a matter of conscience you obviously have to decide for yourself what is to be done. In the future we may see long-tailed Cockers but at the moment the docked tail is a breed characteristic.

Cockers are one of the breeds affected by the 'Fading Puppy syndrome'. No one knows exactly why puppies fade and there may be more than one reason. Some say it is the bitch's milk that is affected; some say a bitch's health that is poor and suspect. There may be many factors, but in my experience the problem of fading puppies appears to be somewhat hereditary. I had a line of bitches and they nearly all had fading puppies. When that line was strengthened with another I had hardly any trouble at all.

The fading puppy will sometimes cry and will not feed as well as the rest of the litter, then slowly but surely it will begin to deteriorate. Very often the bitch pushes the puppy to one side and does not encourage it to feed from her. Almost certainly a fading puppy will die. I have known breeders work for hours and hours on fading puppies with no success at all. My own feeling is that some effort should be made to put the puppy back on its mother's teat in case it is just a puppy out of sorts rather than a fading puppy. Do not be too distressed when a fading puppy dies. Let us hope your bitch has six puppies, three dogs and three bitches, of attractive colouring and that they rear well.

For the first two weeks with her puppies the bitch will need extra food and plenty of fresh water available, with an extra bowl of milk and raw egg added, morning and night. If she does the puppies very well she may slightly deteriorate in condition herself, but careful and proper feeding at this time will assist her to keep in good condition.

The puppies are born blind — that is their eyes are closed. They start opening their eyes at about nine or ten days — a very exciting moment for the breeder.

At about three weeks of age the puppies should be ready for weaning. By that time the mother will be leaving them for long periods and it is now time to introduce them to food. The first meal should be a mixture of warm milk and baby cereal with a little glucose added — not too thin and not too thick. Dip the noses into the mixture and with luck the puppies will start licking and lapping.

Within a day or so scraped meat can be fed to the puppies and they will usually take this with some enthusiasm. Within a week the puppies should be nearly fully weaned from the bitch, but they will still feed from her if she makes herself available.

At the weaning stage feed the mother away from the puppies and keep her from them until she has digested her food or you will find she will eat and go back to her puppies and regurgitate her food for them to eat. If this does happen there is no need to be worried. It is perfectly natural but it is undesirable because at this time the bitch needs nourishment to build herself up again, and if the puppies take it all from her she will not maintain her condition.

From about four weeks of age the daily diet for a litter of Cocker puppies needs careful preparation and needs to be followed closely:

> 5 meals a day until 3 months old.
> 4 meals a day from 3−5 months.
> 3 meals a day from 5−8 months.
> 2 meals a day from 8−12 months.
> After this one main meal or two to maintain
> good health and condition.

The meals should be two milky feeds a day of warmed milk, with raw egg added once a day, and the mixture thickened with a high quality baby cereal. A puppy needs two cooked meat meals daily, mixed with a good quality puppy biscuit meal. Good quality canned meat can be used for these meals if more convenient, but at least one meal a day should be raw meat cut up into small lumps.

Porridge can be used occasionally for a milky feed, sweetened with a little glucose, and boiled fish (boned) can take the place of a cooked meat meal, just to vary the diet a little.

Fresh water must be available at all times and providing your Cocker does not get overweight it does no harm to have a bowl of hard dog biscuit for a youngster to try his teeth on − it saves chair legs and slippers being chewed.

Always maintain strict hygiene with your puppies from the time they are born. If the puppies are whelped on newspaper, which is a very convenient bedding, clean out the paper at least four times a day. Lay the paper down flat, two pages thick, and then shred more newspaper on top. It is warm, clean and easily disposed of.

The puppies should be registered at The Kennel Club when they are four weeks old. Registration forms will be sent to you on request with full details of how to register and the fees to pay. If you intend to breed again it might be worthwhile to register a kennel prefix, but if this is a once-only litter it may not be worthwhile to register a kennel name at The Kennel Club.

If you decide to keep a puppy leave your choice as late as possible. Decide whether you want a dog or bitch — and decide on colouring etc. and, of course, with the experience you have now gained, go for breed points.

The rest of the litter has to be sold and I suggest you consider an advertisement in the dog papers. This is not cheap but usually brings you a good quality enquiry. Also advertise in the local paper. Always put the price in any advertisement and always charge a fair amount to pay for all your expenses. Do not sell puppies cheaply. You know what you paid for your Cocker and you can easily find out the going rate for puppies — charge accordingly. If you include the price in your advertisement you avoid taking dozens of calls from people wanting puppies for next to nothing, and these are rarely good homes. A simple advertisement will do:

COCKER PUPPIES FOR SALE:

Well reared dogs and bitches, (put colours)
Price:
Your name:
Address:
Telephone No.

If you get visitors looking at the puppies and wanting to reserve one take a deposit and ask for the balance to be paid when the puppy is collected at eight weeks of age. Just as you might expect a prospective puppy owner to ask questions, ask a few yourself.

Why did they decide to have a Cocker? Have they had any experience of puppy rearing? What have they prepared for the puppy? Is the garden escape-proof?

How to hold a puppy

If you receive enquiries from abroad for a possible export, the procedure for despatching a puppy out of the country can be quite complicated and I do suggest dealing with a responsible and reliable dog exporter. There are many advertised in the dog papers and they take a burden off your shoulders. You should only send good, sound and typical stock abroad and the price should be exactly the same as you are getting for home sales, adding a little for the extra time you might have to keep a puppy with you and for any injections or veterinary examinations it might have to have.

Do not sell your puppies under eight weeks of age and sell with care. Make sure the buyer knows what he or she is letting themselves in for. Make sure they have the time to spend with the puppy for training and so on. If you have any doubt whether the buyer is a proper person to have a puppy be firm and say no, and suggest they should think again.

It is sad to record that one of the major Cocker clubs in Britain runs a very busy rescue service for unwanted Cockers. There is evidence that many Cockers end up unwanted and go from home to home, finishing in an animal rescue shelter. Do not add to this sad scrap heap. Do your best to place your puppies where they will be well cared for.

The Show Ring

Most dogs ending up in the show ring were bought originally as pets. Perhaps somebody said somewhere along the way, 'You ought to show that dog — you've got a winner there,' and the seed was set. The Cocker owner visited a dog show and realized very quickly that his pet dog was much better than the winners on parade and, before they knew what hit them, they were in the show ring. It might happen like that but the chances are you will be even more successful with a Cocker if a little planning and thought goes into show preparation.

Any Cocker registered at The Kennel Club can be shown at a dog show. Whether you have a winner on the end of the lead depends on the quality of your dog, and to an extent it is dependent on your attitude too.

There are dog shows in most countries of the world and the majority of these are Championship Shows. If your dog wins the top award in its breed, it is on the way to becoming a Champion. In Gundogs the title is 'Show Champion' as distinct from 'Field Trial Champion' or 'Obedience Champion'. The simple title 'Champion' in Cockers denotes the dog is a Show Champion *and* Field Trial Champion — a difficult feat that *has* been attained by some great dogs in the breed. Britain is one of the few countries to hold dog shows of different levels.

There are 'Matches' held by dog clubs when dogs compete in pairs against each other. This is purely a training ground for dog, handler and novice judges. It is a valuable way of learning the ropes, but winning at this level of showing is not rated by established exhibitors.

During the summer months at garden parties, fêtes and galas 'Exemption Shows' are held in Britain. These are dog shows that are exempt from some Kennel Club rules, though they are licensed by The Kennel Club. This type of show is a useful starting ground since many novice owners will be there with their dogs and no one is looking for a high degree of performance or handling ability. At the Exemption Show pedigree dogs compete against each other for the prizes and it is only at this type of show that pedigree, mongrels and cross-breeds have fun competing together in classes titled 'The Dog with the Waggiest Tail' or 'The Dog with the Best Expression'. No one really takes any notice of wins at Exemption Shows and quite often the judging falls below standard when perhaps a local celebrity with little or no experience of dogs judges the classes. Sometimes, however, very important Championship judges might judge the pedigree classes and then a win or placing becomes a little more meaningful.

British dog shows also have the 'Sanction Show', and this is an important part of dog showing in the U.K. This is strictly for pedigree dogs registered at The Kennel Club. It is for dogs that have not won major awards at Championship Shows and it is restricted to dogs which have not won a certain number of first prizes at shows of higher level.

Most Sanction Shows have twenty or twenty-five classes. There are usually three puppy classes — a mixed dog and bitch puppy class from six months (the earliest age you can show a dog) to nine months; and a separate dog and bitch puppy class for puppies from six to twelve months.

At Sanction Shows the classes are usually all mixed breeds. It would be fairly rare to find a class just for Cockers but you would almost certainly have a Gundog class where Cockers are mixed with all the other Gundog breeds. Generally though at a Sanction Show Cockers find themselves in classes where any breed recognized by The Kennel Club is eligible to compete.

The question the novice exhibitor asks is, 'How on earth can my Cocker be judged alongside a Chihuahua or a St. Bernard? Well the judge, if he is a good one, will have an interest and knowledge (not necessarily practical working knowledge, but certainly an academic knowledge of sorts) of most of the breeds recognized by The Kennel Club (about 120). They all have a Breed Standard and they all have good points and bad points. The all-rounder judge has to assess quickly how many virtues and faults each dog has. Some of the finer breed points are ignored at Sanction Shows and it would be unfair to expect a judge to know every Breed Standard word for word and to have knowledge of the more important breed points of every dog showing under him.

So the showmanship of the dog and handler influences the judge in his decisions. Some big breeders keep well away from Sanction Shows saying they are beneath them, but other breeders use them as training grounds for their young dogs. My first Champion gained her ring experience at Sanction Shows, and while she did not *always* win — very few dogs do — she got used to being handled by different people and mixing with other dogs. She learned to ignore other dogs and to show off to her best advantage. The Sanction Show is a most useful level of showing in Britain and I know breeders from many other countries who envy this type of show.

The next level up of showing in Britain is the 'Limited Show'. This is quite similar to a Sanction Show but there might be five or ten more classes and occasionally Cockers and other breeds have separate classes, where a breed judge might share the judging with an all-rounder judge. The Limited Show allows dogs registered at The Kennel Club to compete with each other, but it is restricted to dogs that have not won a Challenge Certificate at Championship Shows.

We now come to the 'Open Show' — a very popular type of show in Britain. Dogs again have to be registered at The Kennel Club but there is no restriction of entry. Champions can — and do — compete against novices, and sometimes the novices beat the Champions. The number of classes at Open Shows can vary from fifty to three hundred at the larger shows and Cockers are classified separately at very many of these shows and Cocker specialist judges officiate. After competing in the Cocker classes you can enter the 'Variety' classes where, as in the Sanction and Limited Shows, you will be up against other breeds. Classes such as 'Any Variety Bred (or not bred) by Exhibitor'; 'Any Variety Junior'; 'Novice and Open'.

If you want to show your Cocker get a copy of the weekly dog magazines which list forthcoming shows. Send a stamped addressed envelope to the Show Secretary for a schedule of the show and read carefully the description of the classes. The Cocker is a breed well-favoured at 'Variety Shows'. Sadly, some breeds rarely get a look in on the awards, but a good Cocker is usually well in the cards.

The most important show is, of course, the Championship Show. Winning at this level counts enormously and demands respect. A novice dog wants placing carefully into the correct class — for example, Maiden — usually for a dog not previously having won a first prize; or Novice — with a similar restriction. A Cocker puppy under nine months of age should only be shown in a puppy class but at ten months onward, if it is developing well, it might be worthwhile to show it also in the Junior class, which is for dogs and bitches from six to eighteen months.

We have discussed grooming in another chapter and I take it for granted that you would not consider entering your Cocker for a dog show unless it was in tip-top condition — not too fat, not too thin, properly groomed, a nice glossy coat, and so on.

Training a puppy for the show ring can, and should be, fun. Remember, you want your Cocker to show off to the best advantage, so getting your puppy to stand properly is one of the first things to be taught. How strange, you might say, of course my puppy stands properly, but in the show ring your Cocker might have to stand still for up to half an hour and the eyes of the judge might be on him all the time. Remember always that it is the dog catching the judge's eye which has a good chance of the top prize. So teach your Cocker to stand up and stand still. Place the front and rear legs in a natural position, neither too drawn out or too close together. Always make sure feet are neither turned in or out. Kneel down by the side of your dog with your right hand touching his chin, giving a little tickle now and again, while the left hand is under the tail encouraging it to be 'merry'. If your puppy can do without your hands in place so much the better, but first of all physical contact with your puppy will give him confidence and he should soon enjoy showing off, and stand correctly.

Encourage members of the family and people he knows to open his mouth gently and look at his teeth; to feel over his head; neck;

body and legs. This is what the judge will do later, but the more your puppy gets handled, the more confidence he will have when he gets into the ring.

You can start training your puppy for the show ring from about four months of age but treat it all as a game. Never take training too seriously at the beginning and never reprimand your puppy too strongly if he puts a foot wrong. If you upset him at this stage you forfeit the chance of him being happy in the show ring later. An unhappy dog rarely wins prizes.

After standing him, and allowing someone to touch him all over, it is time to walk correctly. Walking is important because dogs are judged on their movement and if it is not correct they will find themselves apart from the prize winners. The Cocker's movement is a driving one; moving forward briskly in a positive way, but not running. The movement should be true, meaning that the front and back feet move forward in a straight line, neither too close together or too far apart, and the tail must not be clamped down. Your Cocker should have his head raised. Discourage him from sniffing on the ground, though this is a great temptation especially out of doors. I like to see a Cocker moving on a slack lead, not one that is 'choked' by a taut lead. Keep an eye on movement all the time — remember you are showing off the dog, not yourself, and as long as you do not fall down or bump into anyone it does not matter how you walk. It does matter about the dog at the end of the lead. If your Cocker ever limps or goes lame try and discover the cause immediately because a lame dog must never be shown in the show ring.

Right! If your puppy stands correctly and allows people to touch it, and if it moves in a straight line soundly with a merry tail, it ought to be ready to win a top prize at the next Championship Show! But, before you take your Cocker to its first show, go to one yourself that preferably has Cocker classes and see how others do it. Watch the handler of the dog. See how the judge goes over a dog and how he wants the dog to move. The best way to learn how to show a dog is to watch those most proficient at it, and do the same.

Choose a nearby show for your first; you do not want a long journey which might upset your dog. Arrive at the show at least thirty minutes before you are due in the ring and allow your dog, and yourself, time to settle down. Keep your dog clean. What point is there in hours spent on preparation and grooming your puppy for the big occasion and losing all the gloss in five minutes at the show, when your puppy finds a lump of offensive substance to roll in? Take a small blanket and persuade your dog to lie down. Just before you are due in the ring, groom the puppy through, and as soon as your class is called, in you go!

You will find the ring steward very helpful if you do have a query but try not to bother him or anyone else — concentrate on your dog. Whatever you do never talk to the judge unless he asks you a question — it is forbidden under Kennel Club rules to talk to the judge in the ring.

Those first few times in the show ring are important to your dog. He must enjoy himself. If he misbehaves do not scold him but gently correct whatever he is doing wrong. Try and make sure you are not the first to be seen by the judge and then you can again watch the judge with another puppy and see what he expects of the dogs he is judging. Some judges like to go over Cockers on the floor, but many prefer the Cocker on a table. Part of your training should be to ensure that your puppy is as happy and comfortable standing on a table as standing on the floor.

The judge usually approaches the dog from the front looking at the 'bite' and opening the front lips to see the teeth. He then feels over the head, checking the skull for any signs of coarseness; down the neck to feel the length, and he might put pressure just over the shoulder to see if the front legs stay firm, as they should do, or bow out. He feels the shoulder and runs his hands over the back and over the rear legs to check angulation and he will probably lift the tail and step back to see the overall shape of your dog.

You will then be asked to move your dog. Some judges want you to go straight up and down in the ring once, some may want you to move up and down twice. You may even be required to walk a large triangle so that there can be proper assessment of rear movement going away from the judge and then side movement, and finally front movement as you finish your triangle walking towards the judge. Judges have their own ideas about how to assess the movement of dogs, which is why it is a good idea to watch the judge with other dogs before it is your turn. When moving with your dog make sure you do not come between the judge and your dog. The judge needs an uncluttered view of your dog all the time and when he is watching him sideways on be sure you are the other side of your dog.

After you have moved your Cocker to the judge's satisfaction he may ask you to stand still in the middle of the ring and he might walk all around your dog assessing his position and natural stand. The judge might have a squeaky toy and try to distract your dog. This is frowned upon in the Cocker ring, but the judge can do anything he likes to assist him to assess your dog; he has few rules to abide by.

When the judge has finished with your dog you may have to stand in line for quite some time until he has seen all the dogs in the class. By all means relax your dog if the judge is not looking at him, but a Cocker is expected to be alert at all times and the judge expects him to look the part while he is in the ring.

Never be nervous yourself in the ring — you will transmit your nerves to your dog. Talk to other exhibitors while you are waiting for the judge to finish judging each individual dog, but make sure your dog is not a nuisance to other dogs in the ring.

When the judge has seen all the dogs you will have to get in line and show off again with the others and this is where the training comes in. If your Cocker has a good shape and stands naturally well you have a good chance of attracting the judge to your dog. Judges usually select five or six dogs to stand in the middle of the ring, from which they will make up their final positions. If you are among the lucky five or six you are a step closer to winning an award, but if you are left out, wait until the ring steward or judge says he is finished with you before you leave the ring.

Whatever you do try not to let your emotions show when you leave the ring. No one likes a newcomer to make any comment when leaving the ring. If a ringsider says, 'Hard lines you should have won,' do not say, 'Yes, I think so too. What a rotten judge he was.' Just smile, agree inwardly with the ringside comment but say nothing.

But, of course, you followed my training hints; your dog

Table

"New" dogs (unseen by Judge)

Handler

Dog being examined by Judge

Judge

"Old" dogs (already seen by Judge in a previous class)

Table

Judge

All dogs

"Once round, please"

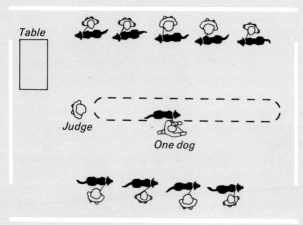

Table

Judge

One dog

"Once up and down, please"

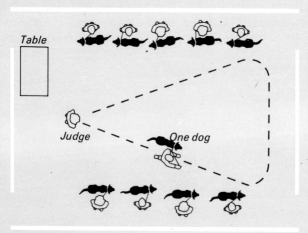

Table

Judge

One dog

"Triangle, please"

71

behaved perfectly standing and moving, and you are one of the lucky ones left in the middle of the ring awaiting your final placing. Never take it for granted you will win a class. The judge has not made his final decision until the steward calls out the winning places, so keep your dog on his toes until the cards are actually handed out.

How can you tell if your dog really is a show standard specimen? I cannot tell you here and the results of just one dog show will not necessarily indicate the show worthiness of your Cocker. You will have to enter a dozen shows under a dozen different judges before you are able to assess the show potential of your dog.

You may have to go to half a dozen shows or more before you win a fifth prize, or you may win a first prize at your very first show. Dog showing is as unpredictable as any sport. By all means start off by thinking you have a Champion, but do not be too disappointed if it turns out that your dog will never win a first prize.

At my very first show with my very first dog I came fifth in a class of five and my prize was a tin of flea powder. I was at a loss to know whether this was a hint to me or my dog! Two years later, I was the proudest man in dogdom when I handled that same dog at a big Championship Show to win her third Challenge Certificate and her title of Champion — and, honestly, if it could happen to me, it could well happen to you.

The Field Trial

I fully appreciate that the majority of readers might own a Cocker but will never work it with a gun or take it to compete in a Field Trial. Perhaps very few Cockers will do the job they were created for, but I hope it will still be of interest to learn a little of the Cocker at work.

The Cocker Spaniel had a job to do. He was created to help his master at the hunt and at the shoot. To demonstrate this fairly unique talent among dogs, Working Field Trials were organized as far back as 1864, when a series of tests showed the ability of the Gundog to do his job properly and efficiently. Cockers were not eligible for the first Field Trials (probably on account of their size) — they were thought of as too small to work the game. How wrong that thinking was!

Spaniels first worked in Field Trials at the turn of the century and they soon came strongly into popularity showing that the Setter and Pointer, whilst excellent at their job, were not as versatile as the Cocker. In the field the Cocker proved himself to be an all-purpose dog. He works well with the sportsman to find game, flush it and retrieve on command. The Cocker is an excellent swimmer, and it is rare to find one that will not eagerly take to water. In fact there are stories of shoots during cold weather when the Cocker was the only dog willing to enter the water for game.

The Cocker has a natural instinct for his work but, of course, careful training by an experienced person is essential for entry into a Field Trial.

For a start the young puppy has to learn to retrieve an object — it can be a ball, an article of clothing or a soft toy, and to bring it back to his owner. This training can only be done by kindness.

Like training for the show ring, it will only be successful if the dog enjoys what he is doing. The puppy (at say four months or so) might run for the ball or toy and then carry it off to chew into pieces, but it you move away from him calling his name, he will be encouraged that way to bring the object to you.

In training, if you throw the object away further each time, it will teach the dog to seek and find, but never let the young Cocker get bored. When he loses interest in the game it is time to pack up and leave the training session to another day.

You could not take a puppy straight to a field where guns are firing every few seconds — the young Cocker has to get used to gunfire and whenever a gun is fired the puppy must learn to drop wherever he is. The command 'drop!' must always be given to a novice dog when a gun is fired, but the Cocker soon learns to drop without the command after a time.

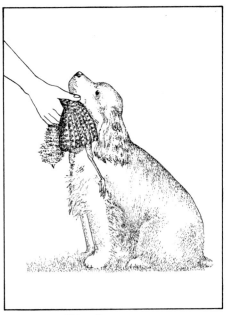

The command 'drop!'

It is essential, of course, that your Cocker never chases game or any small animal in a field. A good way of preventing this is to find someone with a pet rabbit in a pen or run and gently restrain the Cocker when he tries to pounce on the rabbit. The same goes for a running bird; partridge tend to run across the ground or fly very low, and the occasional lazy pheasant will also run across open ground. The command 'drop!' is an important one at this time and you can imagine that a disobedient untrained Cocker would not be a welcome dog at any shoot.

Cocker Spaniel Gun Dog

The title of Field Trial Champion is a much valued and respected one and the dog that gains a full Champion's title — a combined Field Trial Champion and Show Champion — earns admiration all round for his beauty and talents.

Unless you are a member of a shoot, or have a great deal of experience, it is best to have your dog properly trained by an expert for Field Trials. This is expensive, and the cost and lack of personal involvement in the training deters many from taking part in Field Trials.

There are also Working Trials for Cockers and the title of Working Trial Champion can be attained by Cockers; and there are also Championship Obedience Tests. The obedience of the dog has got to be of a very high standard for the top shows, but if you are interested in obedience work or Field Trials, The Kennel Club will be pleased to give you full details of nearby clubs.

While you may not make your Cocker into an Obedience Champion it does no harm to take him to obedience classes. There are clubs in most large cities and novice dogs and owners are always made very welcome. It must be said that the Cocker adapts fairly easily to a good standard of obedience. It is a dog very anxious to please its owner and does not have the strong independent will of some sporting breeds. Unfortunately many sporting dogs associated with hunting are very difficult to train, and some are virtually impossible. The Cocker trains fairly easily.

Field Trials are run under Kennel Club rules and a maximum of sixteen dogs compete, with a draw made if there are more than sixteen to decide which shall compete. The dogs are numbered; one judge takes the odd numbers, the other the evens. Each judge has an official 'gun' and when a judge is satisfied with the work of a dog he calls for another and works through all the dogs this way. The other judge then works the dogs and at the end of the second round the judges compare notes and give out the awards with a run-off if necessary.

The faults at a Field Trial are obvious. A dog will lose points if it slushes game too far away from the gun, and if it misses game when retrieving. A judge has to assess the behaviour of the dog, its scenting ability, its fast response to commands, and so on. A dog must never hold on to its retrieve; it must give up the game willingly to its handler and never place it on the ground.

Whatever game is retrieved must never be marked or damaged in any way. Cockers have a reputation for having soft mouths and I remember seeing one favourite at a famous kennel happily carrying an egg around in her mouth for a long time without cracking the shell.

Field Trials and Working Trials are just demonstrations of a dog's natural working ability, but training is essential for success. In the beauty show ring sometimes an absolutely natural shower could win through to top awards. It could never happen in quite the same way in the field. The 'natural' dog will have an easier time than one who has to be intensely trained, but the inexperienced Cocker at a Field Trial could be dangerous and would soon be shown the gate leading out of the field.

Sitting obediently

Famous Dogs and Kennels

In a handbook such as this it is quite unusual to write about famous dogs and kennels. This is meant to be a very practical book for the new owner of a Cocker and does not pretend to be a breed record of show wins and pedigrees and Challenge Certificate winners. However, certain Cocker Spaniels and kennels have wielded great influence in the breed. There is a strong possibility that you have a Cocker Spaniel puppy because of a famous Cocker named Tracey Witch of Ware, even though she died many years ago.

She won fifty Challenge Certificates. There have been Cockers that have won more than this, but Tracey Witch went better than anyone else. This very beautiful blue roan won Supreme Champion at Cruft's Dog Show — twice! First in 1948 and then at the next Cruft's Show in 1950. There was no show in 1949 and who knows what Tracey Witch would have won at that show! Winning Britain's top dog prize twice has never been done by any other dog in history. Just imagine, first beating every Cocker bitch in a high entry, then beating the best dog, then winning the Gundog group containing some of the best specimens in the world, and then beating every group winner to gain Best in Show at Cruft's — and then doing it all again a couple of years later!

I never had the honour of seeing Tracey Witch of Ware, but my wife saw her win one of her Cruft's 'Best in Show' awards and says she was perfection in a dog. She was in absolute harmony with her owner, the famous Mr. H.S. Lloyd, whose father founded the 'of Ware' kennels back in 1875. If you trace not your Cocker's pedigree but the pedigree of his breeder, you may well find that the breeder or someone along the line came into Cockers because of Tracey Witch of Ware.

Mr. Lloyd's winning at Cruft's was quite incredible and I doubt that it will ever be repeated. He won Best in Show at Cruft's in 1930 and 1931 with Lucky Star of Ware; in 1938 and 1939 he won Best in Show again at Cruft's with Exquisite Model of Ware. There were no Cruft's shows during the war years and 1948 saw the re-introduction of the show and, as I have said, the Supreme award went to Tracey Witch that year with a repeat at the next Cruft's. The Best in Show award at Cruft's is the dream of a lifetime for anyone. Mr. Lloyd and his Cockers did it again and again and again.

Head of Cocker Spaniel

A famous dog I knew well, and often competed against but never with great success, was Champion Lucklena Musical Maid, a very attractive light-blue bitch owned by Mr. Mansfield. She won her show title and then went on to gain her full title by winning at Field Trials. She was very beautiful and again there was perfect understanding between her and her owner. Mr. Mansfield always struck me as a very gentle man, deeply fond of his dogs but also interested in other breeds. His 'Lucklena' kennels are world famous for quality and type.

Front view of a Cocker Spaniel

Side view of black and white Cocker Spaniel

It is interesting to note that many famous breeders and Cocker kennel owners have become well-known International dog show judges. The English Cocker is quite a basic dog without excessive exaggeration anywhere and when you know your Cocker thoroughly you probably learn more about dogs than if you have a breed full of exaggerated points.

Joe Braddon is one of the top judges of all breeds in the world today — his 'Ide' kennels produced many famous Cocker Champions of different colours. Judy de Casembroot who owned the 'Treetops' Cockers is again a famous and well-respected all-rounder judge.

Mr. A.W. Collins' 'Colinwood' kennels has had great influence on the breed, as has the 'Sixshot' kennels of Veronica Lucas-Lucas, and the 'Nostrebor' kennels of Mrs. Robertson.

One of the most famous Cocker breeders of the post-war years has been Miss Macmillan of the 'Lochranza' kennels who went into partnership with Mrs. Gillespie. Dozens of Champions have come from this kennel, which is noted for quality, type and show-manship. John Gillespie has handled many Champions in the show ring and he must be regarded as one of the best handlers of the post-war period. As I write, this Show Champion Lochranza Man of Fashion is just hitting the headlines, one of many dogs belonging to this kennel making his mark as a show winner and dominant stud.

There are dozens and dozens of registered Cocker kennels at The Kennel Club and hundreds of Champions have been made in the breed. I have missed some notable dogs and kennels, but my point is that you may think the show world is far removed from your pet Cocker, but you could be very wrong.

The show world has influenced the size, shape, colour and many characteristics of many dogs. The shape of some dogs has been altered dramatically by the fads and fancies of show judges. This has not happened to the Cocker to any great degree, but I think that great dogs in the breed have influenced people to take an interest in Cockers.

If you ask any prominent Cocker breeder why they started in the breed you will nearly always get the answer — 'Well I saw this dog in the show ring and he was great. He impressed me so much that

I decided there and then that I had to have a Cocker'.

Work it out — if *they* had not started in that way by being influenced by that Cocker, they would not have come into the breed and bred the dogs that are possibly in the pedigree of your own dog — and who knows, if you become interested in showing your Cocker Spaniel, perhaps it too will take its place among the greats in the breed, and you may become a famous and successful breeder yourself. All the famous dogs and people in Cockers had to start somewhere. Usually it was by having just one Cocker and the interest grew and perhaps success came their way, and that was the beginning of it all.

I remember many years ago judging at a small match meeting of my local dog club. A youngster had a Cocker puppy with him and I thought he handled well enough to get my full marks. That youngster was Andrew Caine, who has become one of the top handlers and breeders of American Cocker Spaniels in England. He was one of the first to import stock from America and he was keen enough to learn about the breed in America. His interest began by attending small shows with his Cocker.

Respect the great dogs of the past and the Cocker breeders who have made the Cocker Spaniel what it is today — a dog with few drawbacks and many virtues.

Health

Reading the following list of dog ailments can be a little frightening to the newcomer in dogs, so I must explain that there is every possibility that your dog will go through life free of any of them. Most of my kennel dogs have visited the vet for innoculation against distemper, and never gone again. It is just as frightening to see a list of moving parts in a motor car, but you still happily jump in the driving seat and take a spin without thinking of all that could go wrong.

It is much better with a dog because nature cares for a living animal more effectively than the average motor mechanic cares for a car.

I have to say this because the list of things that can happen to a dog is endless and this chapter is really meant as a dipstick to be looked at occasionally. With most health problems it is advisable to go to your vet. I have had many verbal battles with vets, but I must recommend them rather than going to the pet shop to get medication which may not be effective because in all probability it is not appropriate. By all means read what follows but, remember, not all of these things could happen to your dog!

Abscess: Can be quite painful for a dog. Hot fomentation will bring it to a head and the poison can be squeezed away. Swab with mild antiseptic.

Anaemia: This is usually an iron deficiency and feeding cooked liver will improve the situation. Symptoms may be white gums and the dog may be near collapse. If the condition does not improve within two hours get veterinary assistance.

Anal glands: The anal glands beneath your dog's tail sometimes get clogged with waste matter which irritates the dog and may make him drag his rear end along the ground. If the condition gets serious the vet will empty the glands. With neglect an abscess could form and this can be very painful for your dog.

Arthritis: An old dog may cry out when moving suddenly and be in obvious pain. If the condition is not serious aspirin will relieve the pain, otherwise veterinary treatment is effective.

Bad breath: Can be caused by a multitude of things. Decayed and dirty teeth, mouth ulcer, worms, digestive troubles or kidney disease. Charcoal biscuits help digestive problems sometimes. Veterinary attention to teeth should eradicate the trouble.

Bleeding: Clean any wound with mild antiseptic and examine the extent of the cut. If it needs a stitch get the dog to the vet quickly. If bleeding will not stop get immediate veterinary attention.

Broken bones: If you suspect a bone is broken do not move the dog unnecessarily but get immediate veterinary attention. The worst break will mend with speedy action.

Burns: Keep the dog quiet in a warm dark room. With mild burns use ointment; more serious burns need veterinary treatment.

Canker: The Cocker, unfortunately, is prone to ear canker which usually shows itself with a smelly brown discharge from the inner ear. Get a cleaning oil or powder from your vet and treat as directed.

Car sickness: The dog may drool or vomit after he has been travelling for a few minutes. Avoid feeding the dog for six to eight hours before a long journey. Carry newspaper in case of accidents in the car, but prevention of car sickness is one of just constantly travelling in the car with the dog. Veterinary tablets are a last resort.

Collapse or fainting: Call vet immediately. Remove the dog out of bright sunlight into a warm darkened room. Pull his tongue out to assist his breathing and dampen mouth with water. Do not feed. When dog recovers he is liable to be distressed, so sooth him gently.

Constipation: A teaspoon of liquid paraffin should be effective. Avoid strong laxatives. If dog has no motion for three days call veterinary attention as it may be due to a blockage.

Coughing: Coughing can exhaust a dog and it is wise to consult vet. Check for any obstruction in throat. A bowl of warm milk will do no harm.

Cysts: These can occur round toes of the Cocker. Cut fur away very carefully. Hot fomentation to bring cyst to a head and then mild antiseptic. On the body (if irritating) might need surgery.

Diarrhoea: Might be caused by change of diet; if so, it is no real problem and will clear up. If there is blood in the motion get veterinary advice immediately as it may be enteritis. If diarrhoea persists get veterinary treatment.

Distemper: Symptoms are discharge from eyes and nose, listless, off food, vomiting. Needs veterinary treatment immediately. Distemper often proves fatal and vaccination is the *only* safeguard.

Eating filth and faeces: Usually as a result of vitamin deficiency, so give recommended dose of Canovel tablets. This can become a habit so stop your dog doing this as soon as it is seen.

Eye discharge: Check for dirt or dust in the eye and use eye lotion as directed. If this persists check with vet.

False pregnancy: Nipples sometimes enlarge and fill with milk.

Bitch can go through all the symptoms of real pregnancy including bearing down when puppies would be due. Keep the bitch active to take her mind off her false pregnancy. If the condition becomes unbearable you can get veterinary treatment, but it is best if the bitch can be kept away from the vet for this. Watch out for signs of milk hardening in the breast as this could be serious.

Fits: Get immediate veterinary advice. Place dog comfortably and warmly in a darkened room. The dog may be very frightened when recovered so sooth him gently.

Head shaking: Examine ears to see if they need attention. Check for discharge, heavy waxing, sores or ear mites. Check with your vet to be on the safe side.

Heart trouble: Usual symptoms are panting after walking. Requires veterinary attention, of course, but nowadays a dog can live a useful life with heart trouble, given proper treatment.

Heatstroke: Move dog out of sunlight into darkened room. Put wet cold flannel over head and neck and check constantly. If recovery takes more than an hour check with vet.

Hernia: Fairly common with puppies and rarely needs attention. Usually shows with a 'button' in middle of tummy area. Unless it distresses or irritates the dog veterinary treatment is not necessary.

Kidney trouble: Symptoms are drinking excessively and some-times uncontrollable evacuation of bladder. Tablets from the vet can control effectively. Vet will require a specimen of your dog's urine.

Limping: Check paws for grass seeds or cuts. Feel along the leg to see if dog yelps. If persistent get veterinary attention.

Mammary tumours: A series of hard buttons near teats of bitches. No need for veterinary attention unless they irritate or start to discharge. Can become quite large but I would not recommend surgery unless absolutely necessary.

Poisoning: Suspect poisoning needs fast veterinary attention. A dessertspoonful of salt in a quarter pint of water will act as effective emetic. Keep the dog quiet and warm.

Poor eater: Vary the diet more and ask vet for tonic. Check for worms.

Rickets: Calcium deficiency usually in rearing. Feed bonemeal with main meaty meal. Bones can become mis-shapen but I have seen a very severe case of rickets disappear after effective treatment.

Puppy with rickets

Scratching: Check for parasites and take appropriate action with flea powder from the vets. A flea 'dip' is recommended after bathing.

Skin disease: There are dozens of skin diseases and all require veterinary treatment. Mange shows itself usually by wet sores on the body — this might be infectious so take care. Exhaustive tests sometimes have to be made at veterinary laboratory. In puppies a milk rash is not uncommon, so change diet.

Too fat: Nearly always overfeeding and lack of exercise. Cut down rations gradually and if fatness continues check with vet.

Too thin: Check for worms. Persistent poor eaters usually need veterinary attention.

Vaginal discharge: Could be *Pyometra,* infection of womb, and this is very serious so always check with vet with this symptom.

Vomiting: Most dogs vomit after eating grass and this is of no consequence. Could be an obstruction, so examine the throat. If vomiting persists check with vet for safety's sake.

Whining for no apparent reason: Feel the body all over exerting pressure gently to see if pain can be located. If the dog is obviously distressed get veterinary attention.

Worms: These are a nuisance from birth to old age. Modern worming techniques are effective, harmless and painless, but alwas get worming medicine from vet and not pet shop. If worms are seen in vomit this could mean a serious infestation. Tapeworm is often seen by segments rather like grains of rice around rear end. Worms must have attention quickly because they can affect condition very fast.

First-aid box: Useful items to have standing by:

Aspirin	Eye lotion	Scissors
Bandages	Iodine	Thermometer
Cotton wool	Mild antiseptic	Vaseline
Disinfectant	Ointment (for burns etc.)	Worming tablets

Remember that dogs showing symptoms of any illness should be kept away from other dogs and never take a sick dog to a dog show.

If any symptom is severe get immediate action. The occasional vet bill is a small price to pay to have peace of mind.

Useful Addresses

The Kennel Club, 1 Clarges Street, Piccadilly, London, W1Y 8AB, England.

The American Kennel Club, 51 Madison Avenue, New York, N.Y.10010, U.S.A.

The above will be pleased to send details of clubs involving Cocker Spaniels.

Further Reading

Books:
The Complete Illustrated Cocker Spaniel — Cartledge, J. and L. (eds)
All About the Cocker Spaniel — Gordon, John F.
American Cocker Spaniel Guide — Harmer, Hilary
American Cocker Handbook — Hart, Ernest
Leo C. Wilson on Dogs — Husberg, Kristina and McCarthy, Dennis (eds)
The New (American) Cocker Spaniel — Kraeuchi, Ruth M.

Magazines:
Pure Bred Dogs — American Kennel Gazette, published by The American Kennel Club
Dog World — 22 New Street, Ashford, Kent. TN24 8UX, England.
Our Dogs — 5 Oxford Road, Station Approach, Manchester, M60 1SX, England.

Index